THE
HUMAN
BODY

DO NOT BEND

DON'T GET INVOLVED

SHRIGLEY

DO NOT BEND

REDSTONE

First published 2001
by Redstone Press
7a St Lawrence Terrace London W10 5SU
tel 0207 352 1594 fax 0207 352 8749
www.redstonepress.co.uk

Design: Julian Rothenstein
Artwork: Terence Smiyan Production: Tim Chester

ISBN 1 870003 28 4

A CIP record is available from The British Library

WHAT ARE YOU DOING ?

INTRODUCTION

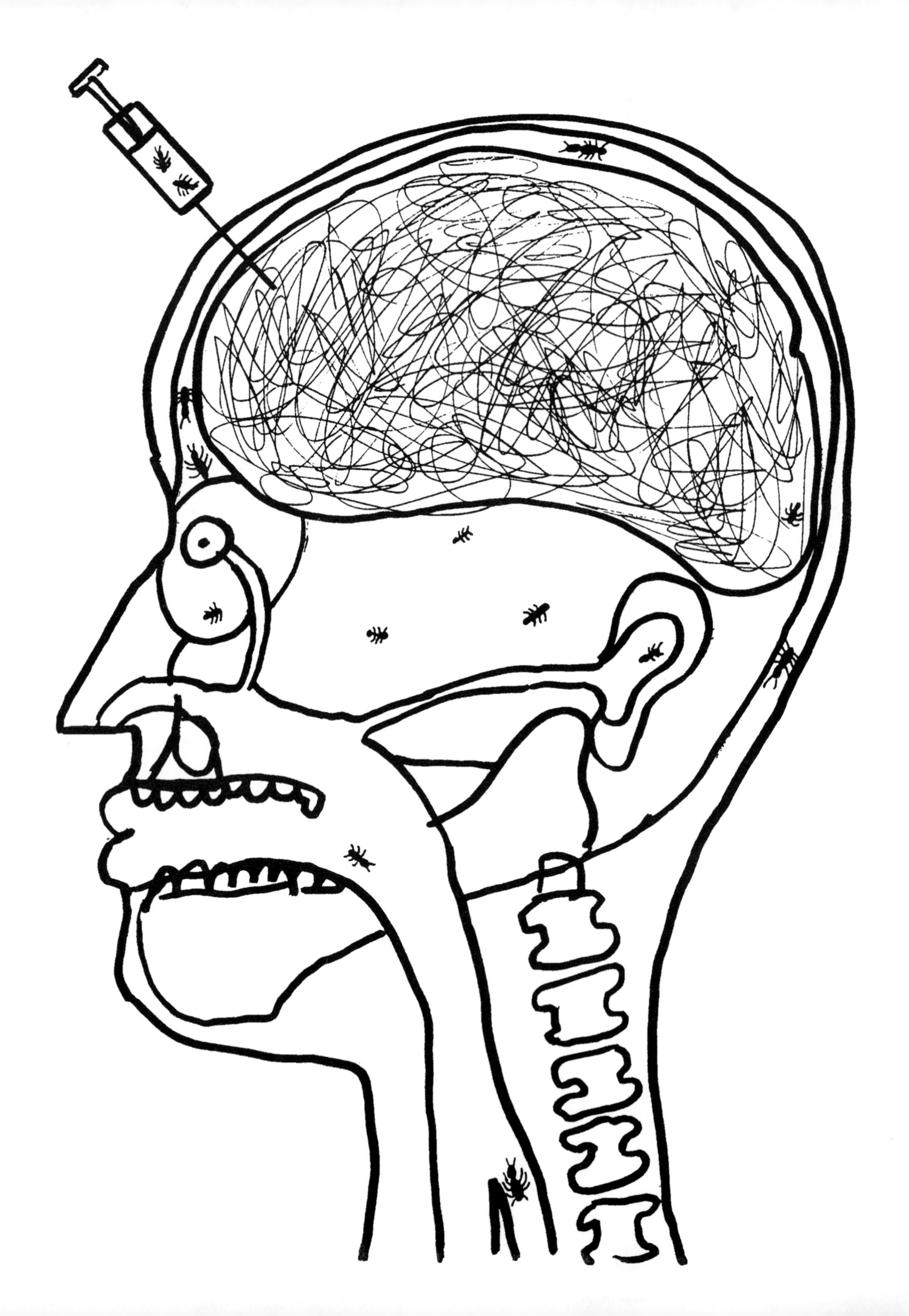

THE DOCTORS

EY REMOVED HIS SPIT GLAND
EY LISTENED TO THE SPARROWS BREAST
EY TORCHED THE GARMENT DISTRICT TO KILL THE MOTHS
EY OPERATED ON HIS HEAD AND TOOK OUT HIS BRAIN
AND WHEN THEY TRIED TO PUT IT BACK IT WOULD NOT FIT
EY BROKE THE LIFE SUPPORT MACHINE
EY HARASS THE GOOD, KIND NURSES
HEY ALL SMOKE AND DRIVE SPORTS CARS AT 100 MPH.
HEY NEVER WASH THEIR HANDS
HEY STUDIED FOR MANY YEARS AND THEY WILL NOT LET US FORGET IT.
EY PLAYED RUGBY WITH A HUMAN SKULL (WHEN THEY WERE AT COLLEGE)
EY FILL SYRINGES WITH
EY PLAY GOLF
EY TATTOO SWEARWORDS ON INTERNAL ORGANS DURING OPERATIONS
EY DO NOT WANT US TO HEAL, NOT FULLY
EY MESS WITH MEDICAL DATABASES
Y DO NOT KNOW THE MEANING OF THE WORD 'STERILE'
EY DRINK WHISKEY FROM TEST TUBES
Y BLOW HORNS, WHISTLES, RING BELLS, SHOUT LATE AT NIGHT, NAKED.
Y BANG DRUMS WITH FIBULAS
Y PLAY ROUNDERS WITH TIBIAS
EY BREAK WINDOWS WITH FEMURS
Y UNBLOCK THE TOILET WITH A HUMERUS
EY MIX DRINKS WITH METACARPALS
EY FIGHT WITH DENTISTS
EY LABOTOMIZE THOSE WHO COMPLAIN
Y BRANDISH SCALPELS LIKE SWORDS
HEY EAT MEAT FROM THE CORPSES BELIEVING IT WILL MAKE THEM STRONG

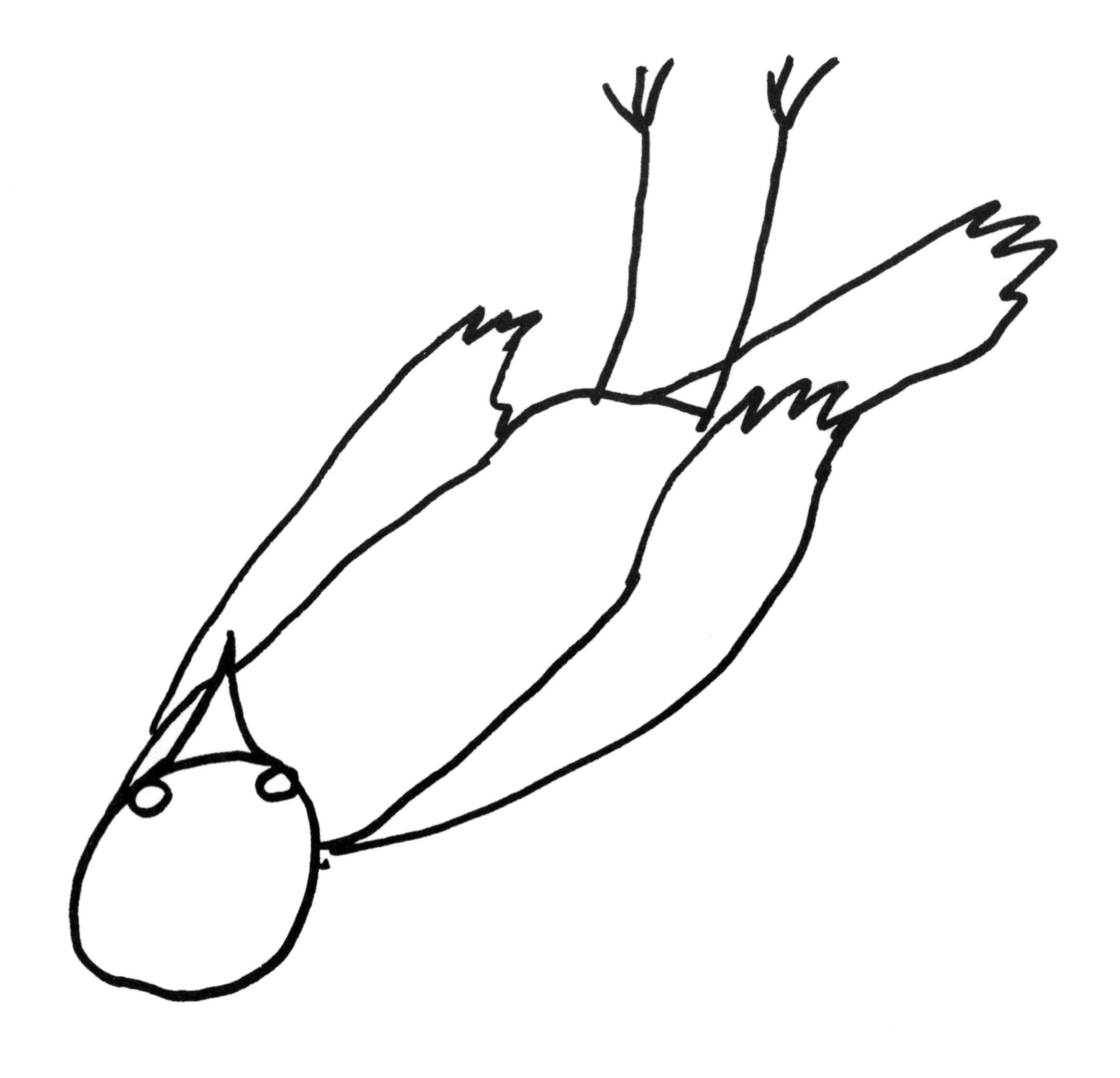

FART

SOWING WILD OATS

UNDER NORMAL CIRCUMSTANCES	UNDER UNUSUAL CIRCUMSTANCES
LION ATTACKS YOU	LION DOESN'T ATTACK YOU
POLITICIAN DELIVERS SPEECH	POLITICIAN REMAINS SILENT
PLANE LANDS SAFELY	PLANE DOESN'T LAND SAFELY
YOU POST LETTER	YOU ARE STRUCK BY LIGHTNING
BEST APPLICANT GETS THE JOB	YOU GET THE JOB (OR SIMILAR DEGENER
DOG BARKS	DOG SPEAKS
DOG WAGS ITS TAIL	DOG WAGS ITS PAW, IN THE SAME AS A HUMAN WOULD WAG THEIR FIN (V. STRANGE)

THINGS I KNOW TO BE TRUE	THINGS I SUSPECT MAY BE FALSE
WHAT IS SAID ON T.V.	HAIR COLOUR
WHAT IS SAID IN THE PAPERS	PROMISES MADE BY GYPSIES
WHAT IS SAID ON THE RADIO	
WHAT I LEARNED AT SCHOOL	
WHAT IS SAID IN THE BIBLE AND ALL OTHER NON-FICTION BOOKS.	

WHAT I THOUGHT THEN	WHAT I NOW KNOW
BAD HABITS MAKE OUR DECISIONS FOR US	GOD USES OUR FAULTS TO FULFIL HIS PURPOSE

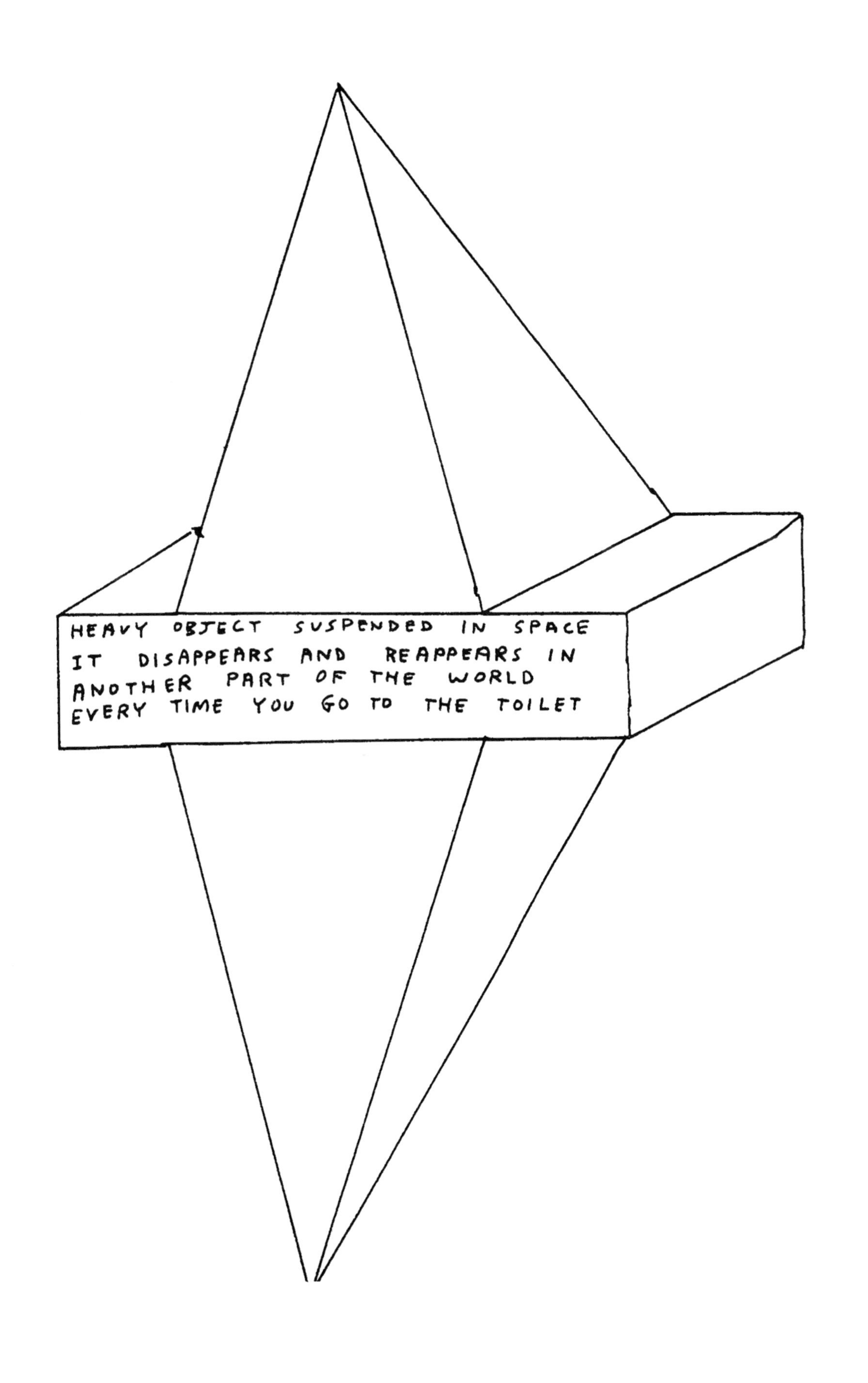
HEAVY OBJECT SUSPENDED IN SPACE
IT DISAPPEARS AND REAPPEARS IN
ANOTHER PART OF THE WORLD
EVERY TIME YOU GO TO THE TOILET

TOM THUMB DESCRIBES SENSATIONS OF BEING IN THESE VASES

PUNK ON A BRIDGE
PUNK JUMPING OFF BRIDGE
PUNK HITS THE WATER
PUNK SINKS TO THE BOTTOM
PUNK DROWNS
PUNK IS DEAD

NUTS

+ COCK

MASHED-UP
+ CHEWED-OFF

HOW CAN I MAKE THE LITTLE FELLOW
UNDERSTAND HOW MUCH I HATE HIS SONG?

OF ALL OF THESE THINGS
YOU ARE THE MOST FUNNY-
LOOKING AND LEAST USEFUL.

FUCK THE WORLD

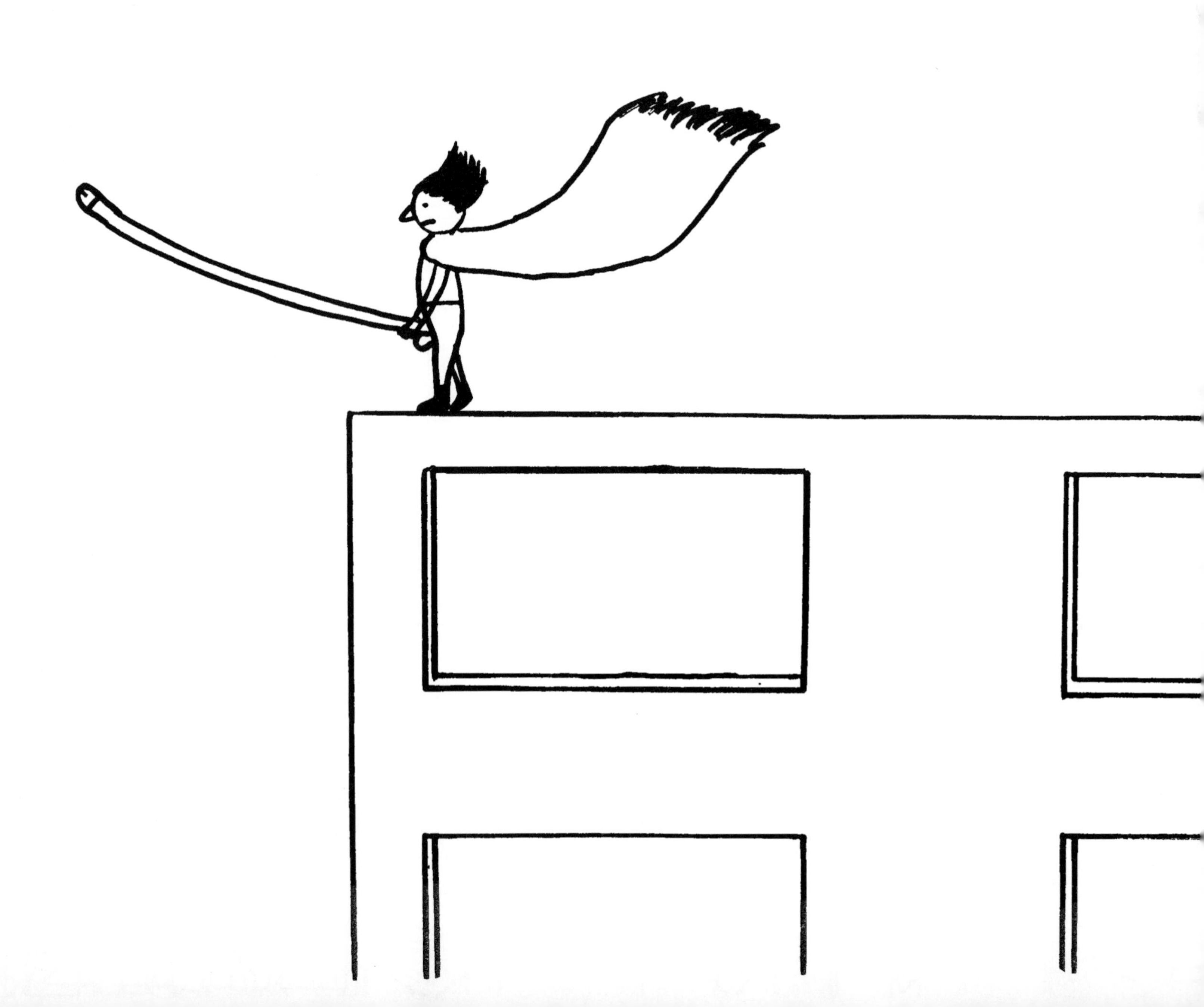

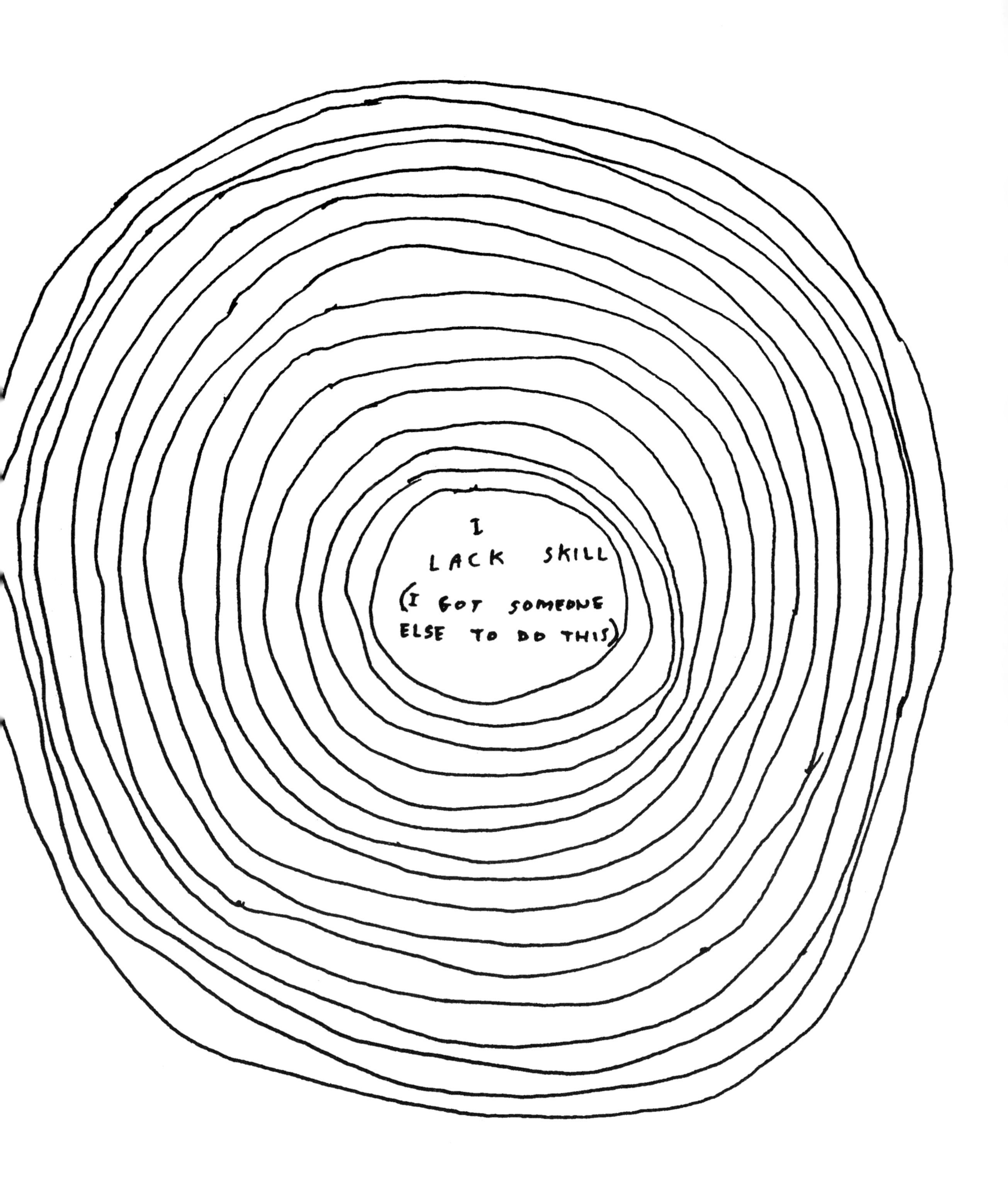
I
LACK SKILL
(I GOT SOMEONE
ELSE TO DO THIS)

COMING SOON

ELEPHANTS

STARRING

2 ELEPHANTS

STAY OUT OF OUR BED. YOU'RE RUINING EVERYTHING.

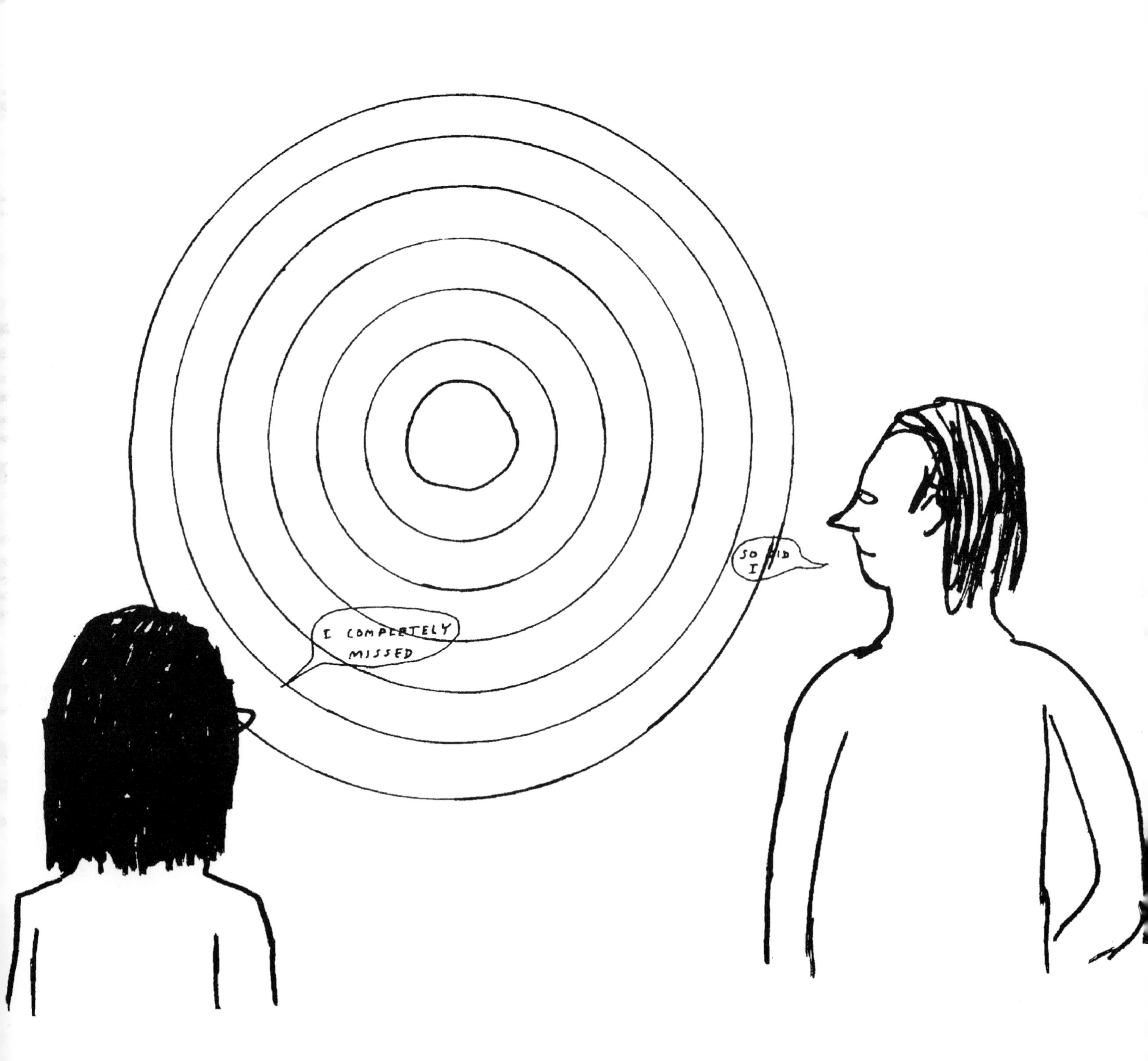
I COMPLETELY MISSED
SO DID I

GANG OF SHE-MEN

DICK
(SUSAN)

GORDO
(JANET)

RODNEY
(MARIA)

BARRY
(MARALYN)

WAYNE
(JANE)

SAMMY P.
(SAMANTHA P.)

SPUD
(VICTORIA)

WATTY
(DOTTY)

DEREK
(BUNTY)

SAMMY F.
(SAMANTHA F.)

FERRET
(FIONA)

PETE
(PETRA)

NIBSEY
(NANNETTE)

AVE
DELLA)

DOUG
(CAROL)

SHUG
(MORAG)

SPAZZER
(SHAZZA)

TOM
(GLADYS)

JONNO
(PENELOPE)

TREV
(MABLE)

IBBLE
SYBIL)

GARY
(MARY)

DOG
(JULIE)

WIGSY
(HENRIETTA)

WEE SHITEY
(CLARISSA)

MALCOLM
(TITTY)

HEIGHT	20 METRES
FACE	2·5 M FROM HAIRLINE TO CHIN
NOSE	70 CM
LIPS	2 M FROM CORNER TO CORNER
BROWS	2·45 M
MOUTH	2 M WHEN STRETCHED AS IN A SMIL
EYES	EACH 30 CM LONG
EARS	30 CM LONG
EYE-TEETH	25 CM HIGH 18 CM AT BASE
MOLARS	36 CM ROUND 12 CM HIGH
CHEST	20 M IN REPOSE
LEGS	5 M
ARMS	8 M
REACH	25 M

MODERN
DANCE

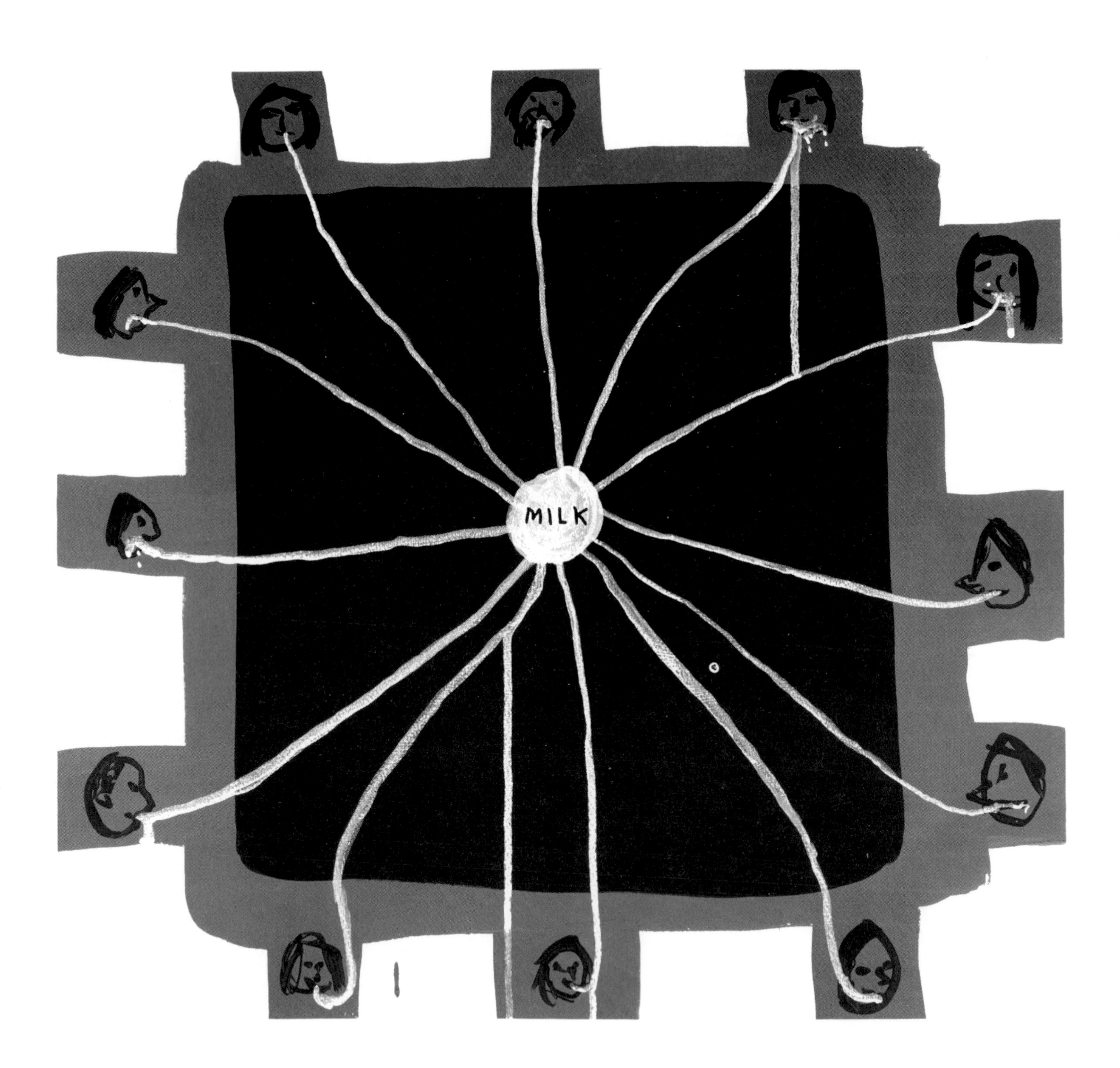
MILK

IS ALL AS IT SEEMS?

JUST A PENCIL OR SOMETHING MORE?

JUST A SACK OR, LIKE THE PENCIL, SOMETHING MORE?

JUST A SEVERED HAND OR, LIKE THE PENCIL AND THE SACK, SOMETHING MORE?

JUST A COCKROACH OR, LIKE THE PENCIL, THE SACK AND THE SEVERED HAND, SOMETHING MORE?

JUST A STICK OF DYNAMITE OR, LIKE THE PENCIL, THE SACK, THE SEVERED HAND AND THE COCKROACH, SOMETHING MORE?

JUST AN ISLAND OR, LIKE THE PENCIL, THE SACK, THE SEVERED HAND, THE COCKROACH AND THE STICK OF DYNAMITE, SOMETHING MORE?

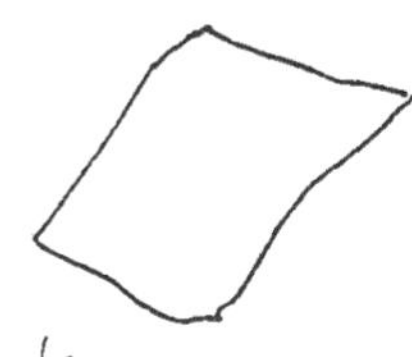

JUST A PIECE OF PAPER OR, LIKE THE PENCIL, THE SACK, THE SEVERED HAND, THE COCKROACH, THE STICK OF DYNAMITE AND THE ISLAND, SOMETHING MORE?

JUST A JUDAS HANGING FROM A TREE OR, LIKE THE PENCIL, THE SACK, THE SEVERED HAND, THE COCKROACH, THE STICK OF DYNAMITE, THE ISLAND AND THE PIECE OF PAPER, SOMETHING MORE?

JUST A THREE-LEGGED CAT OR, LIKE THE PENCIL, THE SACK THE SEVERED HAND, THE COCKROACH, THE STICK OF DYNAMITE THE ISLAND, THE PIECE OF PAPER AND THE JUDAS HANGING FROM A TREE, SOMETHING MORE?

JUST A FUNNY LOOK OR, LIKE THE PENCIL AND ALL THE OTHER STUFF, SOMETHING MORE?

THE REASON FOR THE PEN + NOTEBOOK ON A STRING 'ROUND MY NECK

DURING THE DAY

WHEN I AM OUT WANDERING AROUND THE TOWN I OFTEN HAVE BRILLIANT IDEAS HOWEVER I NEVER WRITE THEM DOWN AND BY THE TIME I GET HOME THEY ARE FORGOTTEN.

CONTEMPORARY ART

NOW I INSULT YOU

"YOU CANAL WATER"
"YOU SECURITY GAURD"
"YOU FAULTY COMPASS"
"YOU EXPIRY DATE"
"YOU FALSE ECONOMY"
"YOU HAIR DRYER"
"YOU CAR ALARM"
"YOU POWER-FAILURE"
"YOU FOOD-POISONING"
"YOU WORST CASE-SCENARIO"
"YOU FRIDGE NOISE"
"YOU SOUND THAT CAMELS MAKE"

"YOU FOOD POISONING"
"YOU LAKE"
"YOU FOOD POISONING"
"YOU FOOD POISONING"
"YOU PROVINCE"
"YOU TOFU BURGER"

NOW I DRAW YOUR MOTHER

"WHAT A BIFFER"

NUDIST DAY AT THE MUSEUM

HE LOOKED
CLOSELY
AT THE THING IN HIS HAND
HE DID NOT KNOW WHAT IT WAS
O HE SHOWED IT
O SOMEONE
LSE
WHO ALSO DID NOT KNOW WHAT IT WAS
I DON'T KNOW WHAT IT IS
SO HE TOOK IT TO THE MUSEUM
BUT THEY WERE BUSY
O HE LOOKED
N THE INTERNET
AND HE FOUND THERE WAS AN EXPERT WHO LIVED IN AMERICA
SO HE SENT HIM AN E-MAIL
BUT HE GOT NO REPLY
O HE SENT
NOTHER E-MAIL
BUT HE GOT NO REPLY
SO HE SENT ANOTHER E-MAIL
BUT HE GOT NO REPLY
O HE SENT ANOTHER
-MAIL
BUT HE GOT NO REPLY
SO HE SENT ANOTHER E-MAIL
BUT HE GOT NO REPLY
O HE SENT
NOTHER E-MAL
BUT HE GOT NO REPLY
SO HE SENT ANOTHER E-MAIL
AND HE GOT NO REPLY.

YOU PRAY BEFORE ABSTRACT SCULPTURE

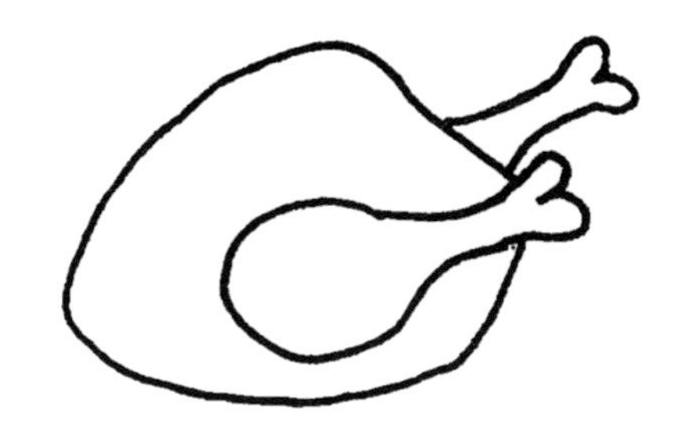

THE BASIC PLOT

A SOLDIER FROM THE OLD ARMY GETS A JOB WITH THE NEW ARMY. HIS JOB IS TO OPERATE THE COMPUTER BUT HE ISN'T VERY GOOD AT IT AND HE MAKES PLANES CRASH AND THINGS. THE NEW ARMY LOSES THE WAR AND THE COUNTRY IS OVERRUN BY BULLIES. ARMY IS DISBANDED AND SOLDIERS ARE FORCED TO LIVE AS SLAVES.

BOIL IN
THE BAG

TRY NOT TO SHAKE SO MUCH

I'M TRYING

WELL TRY HARDER

I'M TRYING BUT IT'S REALLY DIFFICULT

HOW LONG HAVE YOU BEEN SHAKING?

ALL MY LIFE

THAT'S SAD. I WISH THERE WAS SOMETHING I COULD DO TO HELP YOU.

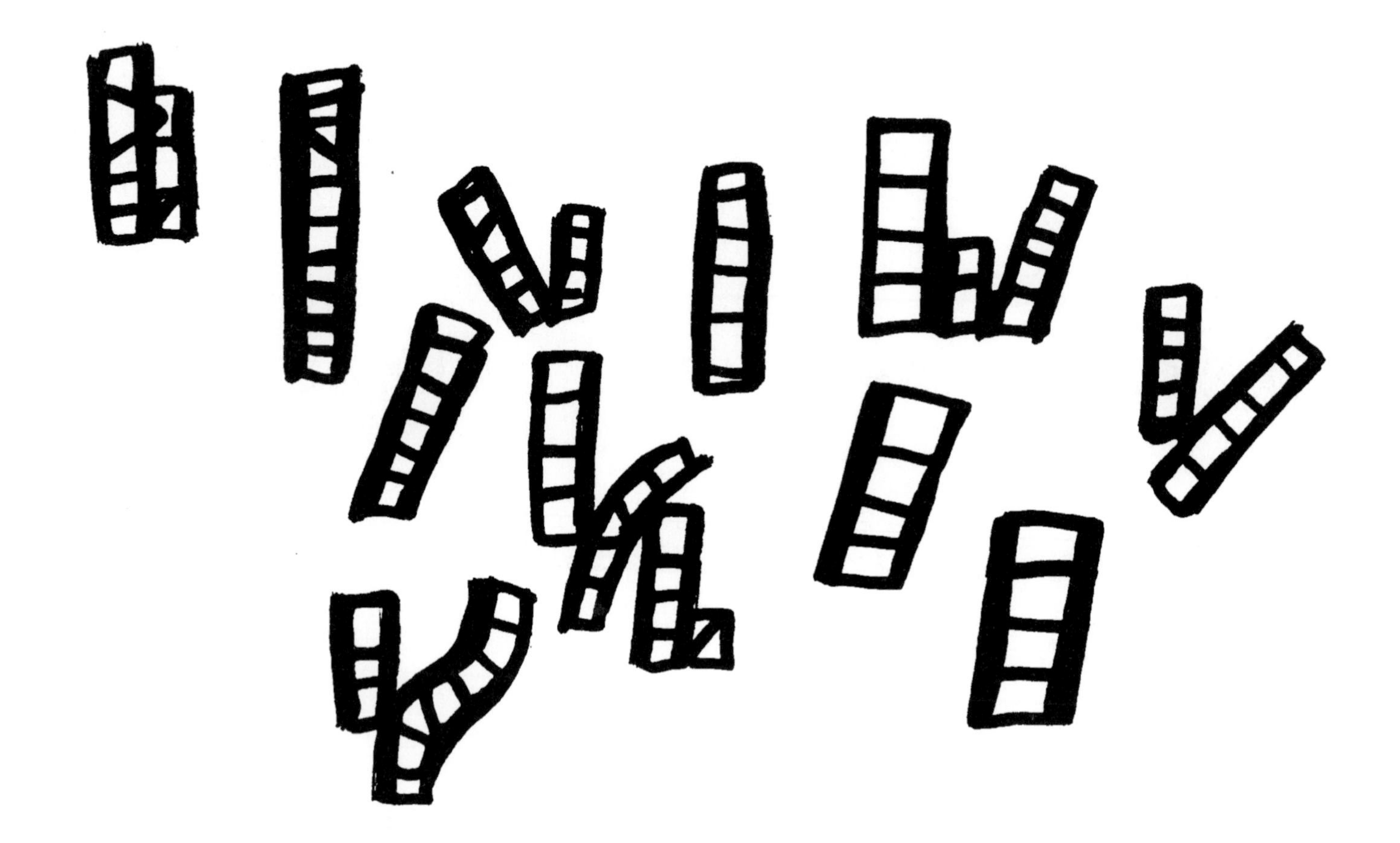

THE ROLE OF THE EDITOR

THE ROLE OF THE EDITOR IS TO REMOVE PIECES OF THE FILM SO THAT IT MAKES BETTER SENSE. THIS PROCESS IS CARRIED OUT IN THE 'CUTTING ROOM'. THE PIECES OF THE FILM THAT ARE REMOVED ARE LEFT 'ON THE CUTTING ROOM FLOOR'. MY FRIEND MARTIN IS AN EDITOR OF DOCUMENTARY FILMS. HE IS A BORING CHUMP.

HOW DID YOU FEEL WHEN YOU READ MY ESSAY 'HOW MEAT GOES BAD'?
I FELT TROUBLED,
AND DID YOU LIKE THE ILLUSTRATIONS?
THEY TROUBLED ME ALSO.
TROUBLED? NEVER MIND, IT DOESN'T MATTER ANYWAY. YOU'D BETTER GO BACK TO YOUR SEAT NOW BECAUSE WE'RE GOING TO CRASH
YES CAPTAIN.

KNOCK KNOCK

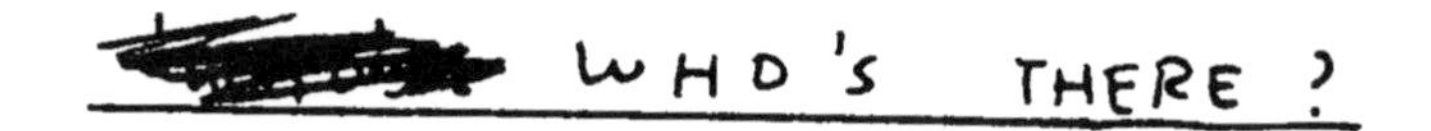

WHO'S THERE ?

IT'S

JOHN, GEORGE, JAN, JACOB, HANS,

HEINRICH, JOSEF, COLIN, CALUM, IAN,

SIMON, STANTON, FINDLAY, LUKAS,

WILLIAM, NELSON, GARY, JEFFERY,

ALAN, KEVIN, KEITH, AND DUANE.

THEY'VE COME TO KILL YOU

AND BURN DOWN YOUR HOUSE.

I HAVE
BEEN DRIVEN
INSANE BY
LOVE

PECKING ORDER

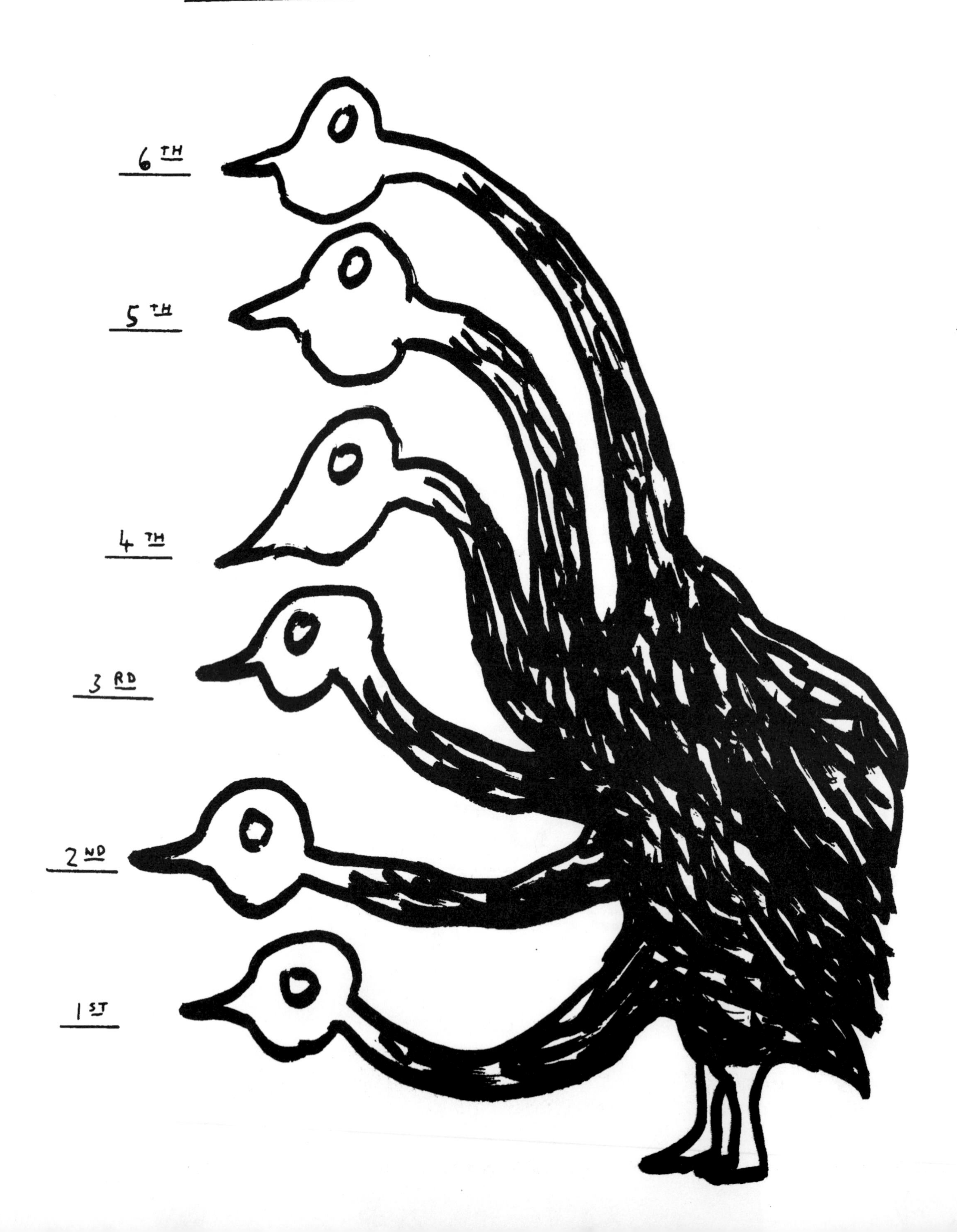

NEW MEANINGS

SOMETHING HAS CHANGED

IT IS NOT THE BIRDS IN FLIGHT
IT IS NOT THE WORMS BENEATH THE EARTH
IT IS NOT THE SMELL OF THE DANISH PASTRIES
IT IS NOT THE TALL BUILDINGS
OR THE ROAD LAYOUT
OR THE TRIFFIC LIGHT SEQUENCE
OR THE BEAUTIFUL WOMEN
OR THE BRUTALITY OF THE AUTHORITIES
OR THE LACKADAISICAL ATTITUDE OF THE POPULUS
OR THE RUBBISH
OR THE PLASTIC CONES

IT IS NOT THESE THINGS IN THEMSELVES THAT HAVE CHANGED
IT IS THEIR MEANINGS THAT HAVE CHANGED.

THE BIRDS IN FLIGHT USED TO MEAN THAT THEY WERE MIGRATING TO A WARMER CLIMATE BECAUSE WINTER WAS COMING.

THE BIRDS IN FLIGHT NOW MEAN THAT HUMAN BEINGS IN THIS COUNTRY ARE INTOLERABLE AND THE BIRDS HAVE BEEN FORCED TO LEAVE TO FIND NICER PEOPLE FURTHER SOUTH.

THE WORMS BENEATH THE EARTH USED TO MEAN THAT THE SOIL WAS HEALTHY AND PLANTS WOULD GROW EASILY. NOW THE WORMS ARE THERE TO REMIND US OF DEATH.

THE SMELL OF THE DANISH PASTRIES USED TO REMIND US IT WAS TIME FOR A COFFEE BREAK. NOW, LIKE THE WORMS, IT REMINDS US OF DEATH.

THE TALL BUILDINGS USED TO BE A MONUMENT TO PROGRESS. NOW THEY ARE DEPRESSING.

THE ROAD LAYOUT USED TO SYMBOLIZE ORDER AND HOW WELL EVERYTHING WORKED. NOW IT REMINDS US OF DEATH.

THE TRAFFIC LIGHT SEQUENCE USED TO INSPIRE SAFETY AND ENCOURAGE SOCIAL RESPONSIBILITY. NOW THEY REMIND US OF DEATH

THE BEAUTIFUL WOMEN, EVERYONE USED TO LOVE THE BEAUTIFUL WOMEN. NOW WE IGNORE THEM.

THE BRUTALITY OF THE AUTHORITIES USED TO BE A CAUSE FOR CONCERN. NOW IT CONSTITUTES KINDESS ON THEIR PART.

THE LACKADAISICAL ATTITUDE OF THE POPULUS USED TO BE INCOMPREHENSIBLE. NOW WE KNOW IT IS CAUSED BY POP MUSIC.

THE RUBBISH USED TO REMIND US THAT THE RUBBISH COLLECTOR WOULD SOON ARRIVE. NOW THE RUBBISH REMINDS US OF OURSELVES.

THE PLASTIC CONES USED TO BE GOOD. NOW THEY ARE BAD.

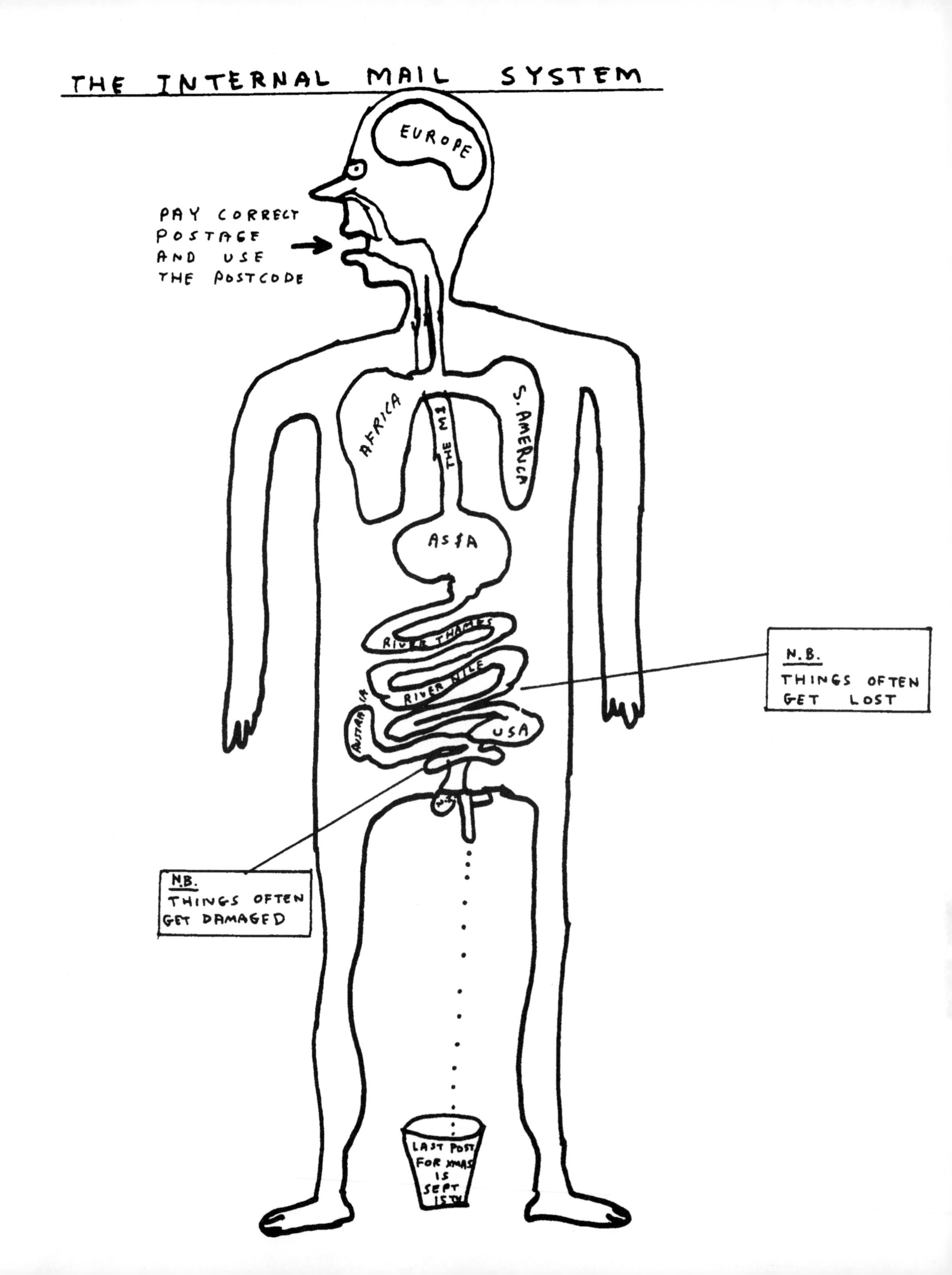
THE INTERNAL MAIL SYSTEM
EUROPE
PAY CORRECT POSTAGE AND USE THE POSTCODE
AFRICA
THE M1
S. AMERICA
ASIA
RIVER THAMES
RIVER NILE
AUSTRALIA
USA
N.B. THINGS OFTEN GET LOST
N.B. THINGS OFTEN GET DAMAGED
LAST POST FOR XMAS IS SEPT 15TH

KILLERS

WHO ARE YOU ?
I'M YOUR SON

- DO YOU RECOGNISE THIS MAN?
- NO
- YOU WILL DO ONE DAY.
- WHY? WHEN?
- WHEN YOU LOOK IN THE MIRROR. HA HA HA HA HA HA HA HA HA HA HA HA HA HA HA HA HA H..... (LAUGHING IS INTERRUPTED BY GUN SHOT)

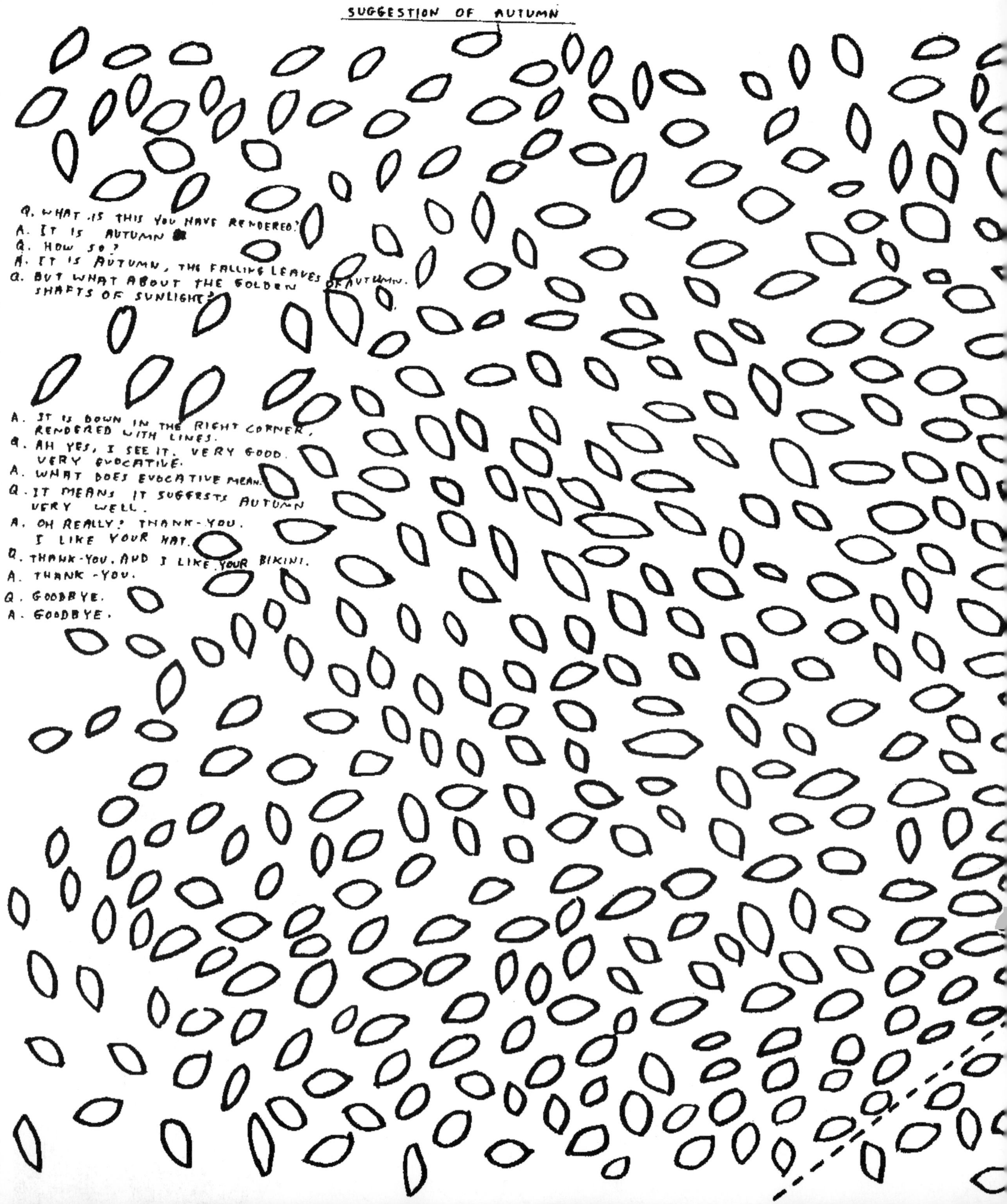

SUGGESTION OF AUTUMN

Q. WHAT IS THIS YOU HAVE RENDERED?
A. IT IS AUTUMN
Q. HOW SO?
A. IT IS AUTUMN, THE FALLING LEAVES OF AUTUMN.
Q. BUT WHAT ABOUT THE GOLDEN SHAFTS OF SUNLIGHT?

A. IT IS DOWN IN THE RIGHT CORNER, RENDERED WITH LINES.
Q. AH YES, I SEE IT. VERY GOOD. VERY EVOCATIVE.
A. WHAT DOES EVOCATIVE MEAN?
Q. IT MEANS IT SUGGESTS AUTUMN VERY WELL.
A. OH REALLY? THANK-YOU. I LIKE YOUR HAT.
Q. THANK-YOU. AND I LIKE YOUR BIKINI.
A. THANK-YOU.
Q. GOODBYE.
A. GOODBYE.

JAZZ

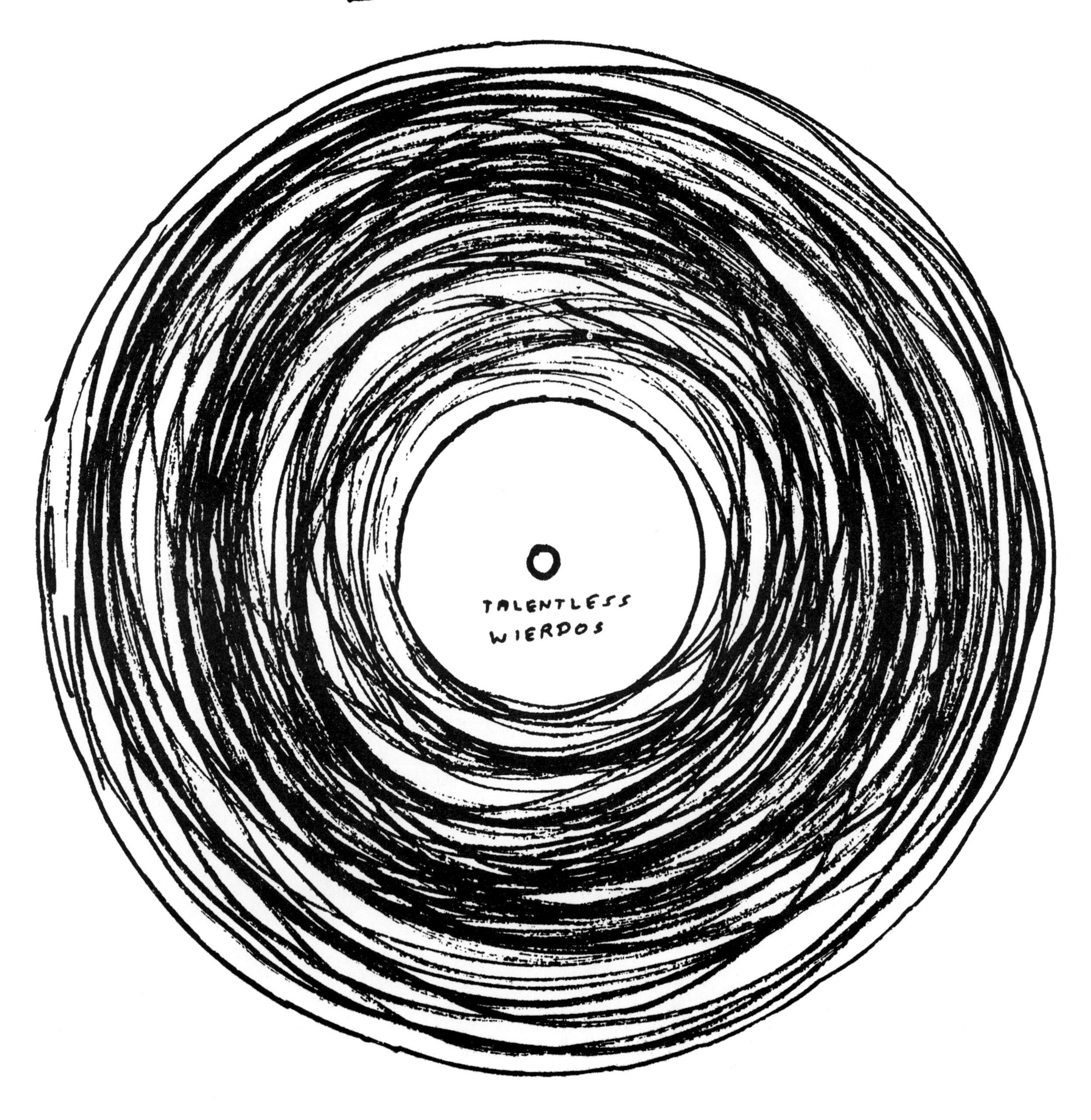

TEXT HAS THE POWER TO CONFUSE, TO MISLEAD AND TO PROMOTE FALSEHOOD. TEXT CAN ILLICIT MANY DIFFERENT RESPONSES : INDIFFERENCE ; SADNESS ; ANGER ; DISAFFECTION AND OTHER EMOTIONS BEST LEFT DORMANT : DANGEROUS LUSTS AND FERVOURS WHICH INVOLVE RITUALS (FIREWORKS, ETC.). TEXT CAN ENGENDER CHAOS. TEXT OFTEN CAUSES WARS AND OIL SPILLS AND PREVENTS CURES BEING FOUND FOR TERRIBLE DISEASES. TEXT DOES NOT HAVE THE POWER TO MAKE PEOPLE HAPPY. ONLY BOOZE CAN DO THIS.

I AM NUMBER ONE
YOU ARE NUMBER TWO
I DO NOT HAVE TO TAKE SHIT
FROM YOU
THE GERMAN GUY IS NUMBER
THREE
YOU DO NOT HAVE TO TAKE SHIT
FROM THE GERMAN GUY
THE RUSSIAN GUY IS NUMBER FOUR
THE GERMAN GUY DOES NOT HAVE
TO TAKE SHIT FROM THE RUSSIAN GUY
THE MEXICAN WOMAN IS
NUMBER FIVE
THE RUSSIAN GUY DOES
NOT HAVE TO TAKE SHIT
FROM THE MEXICAN WOMAN
THE CHICKEN IS NUMBER SIX
THE MEXICAN WOMAN DOES
NOT HAVE TO TAKE SHIT
FROM THE CHICKEN
PETER IS NUMBER EIGHT
THE CHICKEN DOES NOT HAVE
TO TAKE SHIT FROM PETER
THERE IS NO NUMBER NINE

THE D. IS DEAD

D STOP CALLING IT'S NAME. STOP SNIFFING AROUND WHERE WE
D TO KEEP IT. STOP COMING 'ROUND AND LEAVING FOOD. STOP
NDING LITTLE BLANKETS AND THINGS. STOP PHONING US. STOP
ING FOR PHOTOGRAPHS. STOP WRITING IT LETTERS (THAT WAS ALWAYS
INTLESS ANYWAY). STOP REMARKING ON IT'S ABSENCE. STOP ASKING
HERE IT'S GONE. STOP TELLING YOUR FRIEND'S. STOP PROTESTING
, OUR LAND. STOP PESTERING THE AUTHORITIES. JUST STOP STOP
TOP STOP STOP IT. OTHERWISE THIS;

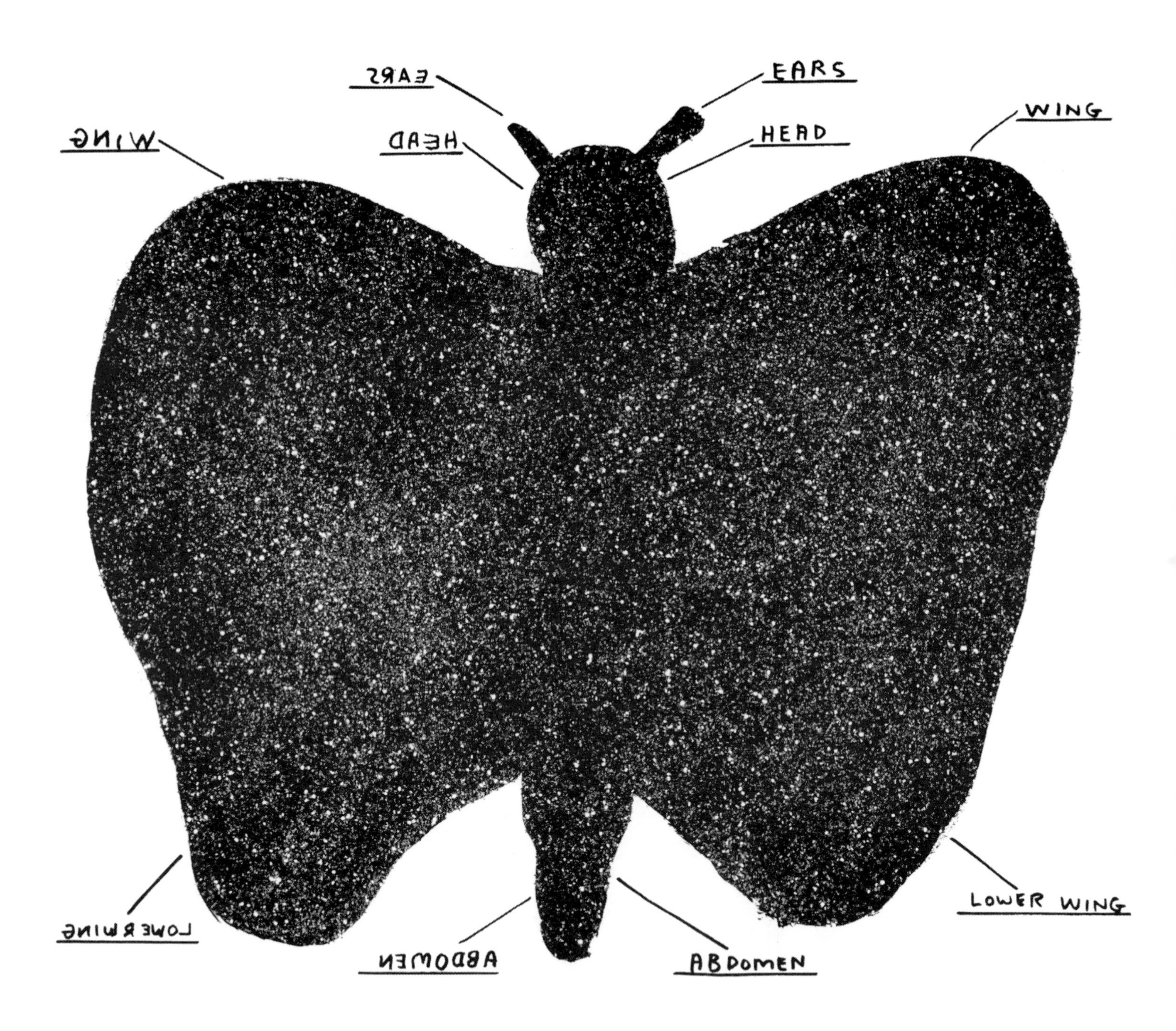
EARS
HEAD
WING
LOWER WING
ABDOMEN

Mood Swings

would you like to come for dinner tonight ?

Fuck off, you whore

FROM NOW ON

I WILL DO

XACTLY

AS I AM TOLD

I WILL NOT DO ANYTHING THAT IS AGAINST THE LAW
I WILL NOT REMOVE ANY PART OF MY CLOTHING
I WILL NOT DO ANYTHING SEXUAL
I WILL NOT DO ANYTHING AT NIGHT TIME (AFTER 5 PM)
I WILL NOT DO ANYTHING OUTDOORS IF IT IS RAINING
I WILL NOT DO ANYTHING OUT OF TOWN
I WILL NOT DO ANYTHING IN THE ROUGH PARTS OF TOWN
I WILL NOT DO ANYTHING WITH RETARDED PEOPLE OR DISABLED PEOPLE OR CHILDREN OR ANIMALS
I WOULD RATHER NOT DO ANYTHING WITH FOREIGN PEOPLE OR PEOPLE WITH STRONG REGIONAL ACCENTS
I WILL NOT DO ANYTHING NEAR LARGE BODIES OF WATER
I WILL NOT DO ANYTHING DOWN MINES
I WILL NOT DO ANYTHING DOWN THE SEWER OR NEAR TO DRAINS
I WILL NOT DO ANYTHING WHERE THERE IS DUST OR DIRT OR INSECTS OR SMELLS
I WILL NOT DO ANYTHING EARLY IN THE MORNING
I WILL NOT DO ANYTHING IN WINTER
I WILL NOT DO ANYTHING IF YOU SHOUT AT ME
I WILL NOT DO ANYTHING IF YOU CALL ME WHAT YOU CALLED ME IN YOUR PAMPHLET
I WILL NOT DO ANYTHING BORING
I WILL NOT DO ANYTHING OBVIOUS OR TRITE OR BANAL
I WILL NOT DO ANYTHING DANGEROUS
I WILL NOT TAKE ANY PILLS
I MUST BE ABLE TO SMOKE CIGARETTES
I WILL NOT READ ANYTHING
I WILL NOT SAY ANYTHING
I WILL NOT DO ANYTHING DEPRESSING
I WILL NOT RENOUNCE MY BEHAVIOUR PREVIOUS TO THIS RESOLUTION
I WILL NOT ENDORSE YOUR OPINIONS (ESPECIALLY YOUR OPINIONS ABOUT ME)
I WILL NOT SIGN ANYTHING (EXCEPT THIS)
I WILL NOT WRITE ANTHING (EXCEPT THIS)
I MUST BE ABLE TO WEAR MY OWN CLOTHES
APART FROM THESE THINGS YOU CAN CONSIDER ME YOUR HUMBLE AND LOYAL SERVANT
I WOULD LIKE TO TAKE THIS OPPORTUNITY TO THANK YOU FOR YOUR KIND OFFER OF EMPLOYMENT AND
INCERELY HOPE THAT I CAN LIVE UP TO YOUR CONFIDENCE IN ME.
BLESS YOU KIND SIR.
OVE YOU.

NO MORE MILK

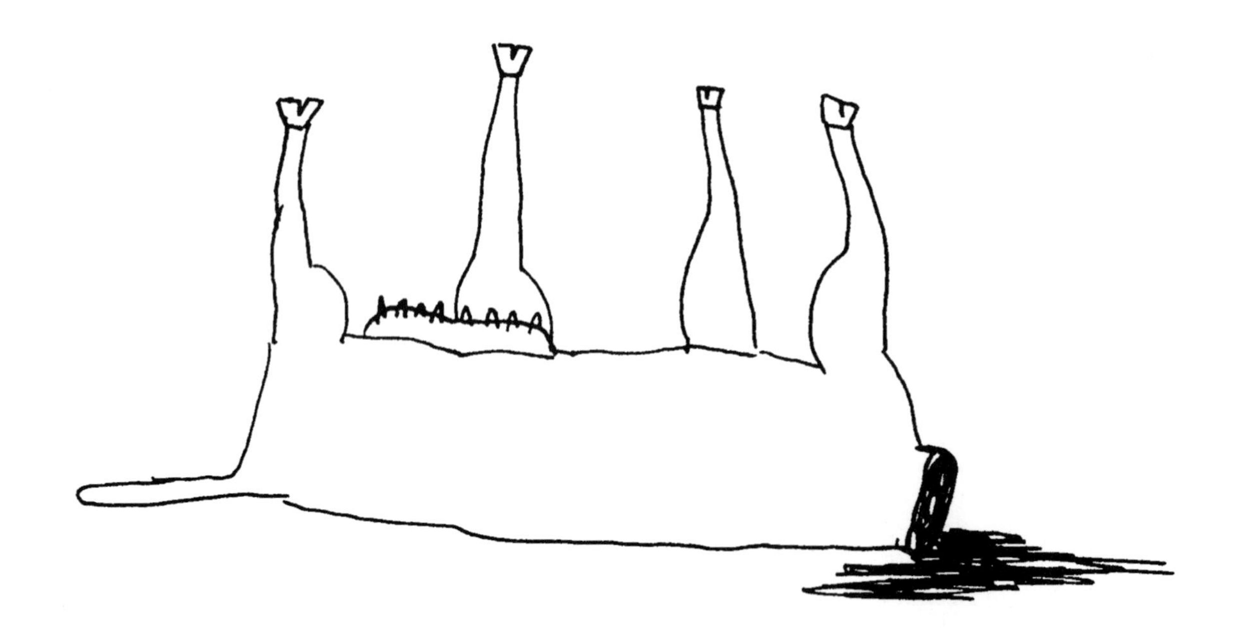

MOTHER!
MOTHER!

MOTHER IT'S ME!

OH! I'M SORRY I THOUGHT YOU WERE SOMEONE ELSE

EXAM
WHAT IS YOUR
NAME?
A. TED
B. BRIAN
C. DAVE
D. SUSAN

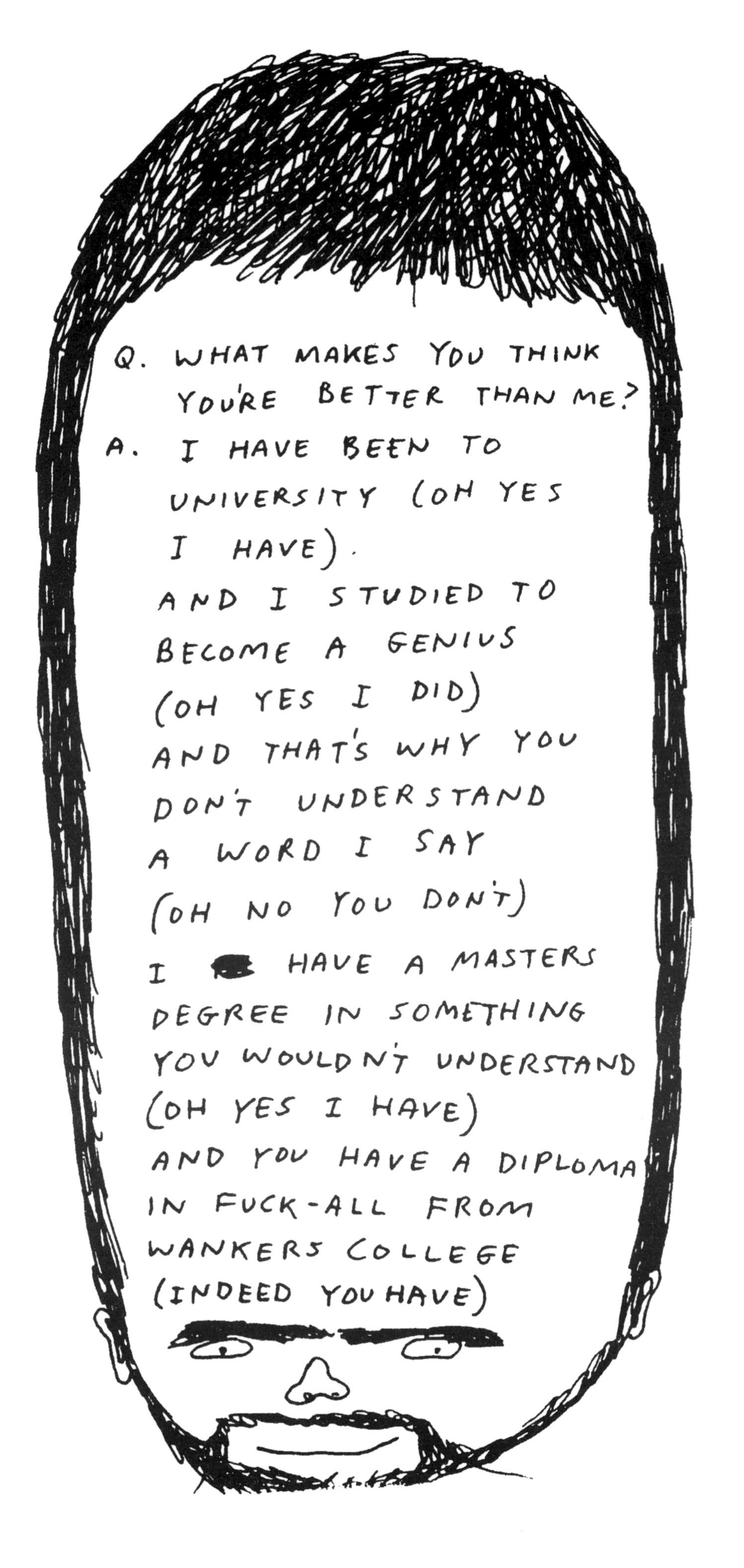
Q. WHAT MAKES YOU THINK YOU'RE BETTER THAN ME?
A. I HAVE BEEN TO UNIVERSITY (OH YES I HAVE).
AND I STUDIED TO BECOME A GENIUS (OH YES I DID)
AND THAT'S WHY YOU DON'T UNDERSTAND A WORD I SAY (OH NO YOU DON'T)
I HAVE A MASTERS DEGREE IN SOMETHING YOU WOULDN'T UNDERSTAND (OH YES I HAVE)
AND YOU HAVE A DIPLOMA IN FUCK-ALL FROM WANKERS COLLEGE (INDEED YOU HAVE)

I TOOK ACID AND
PUKED SPIDERS' WEBS

ThE THE ThE

WorLD OF

THE ThE END

THE ThE END THE

THE The

Th

OF

IT

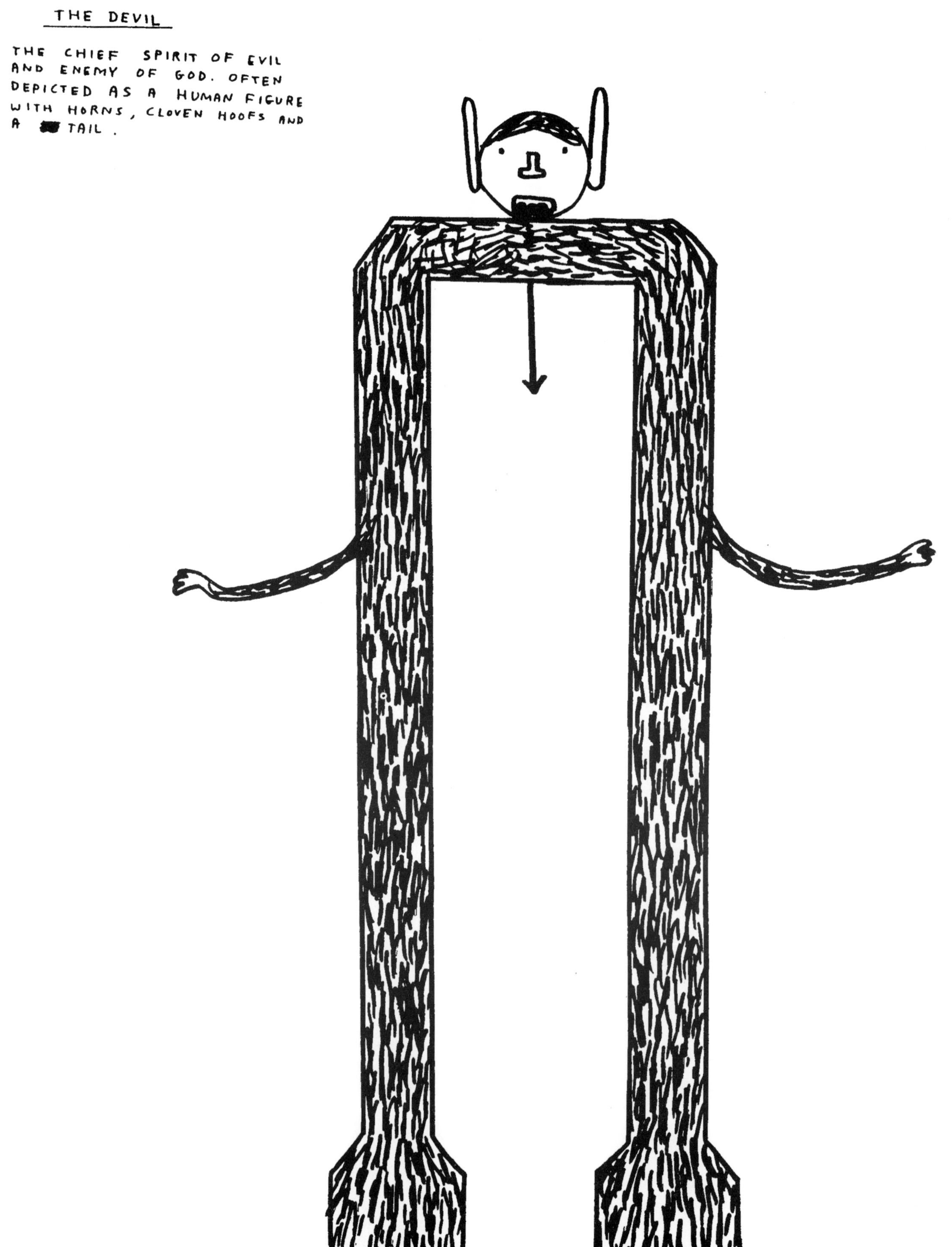
THE DEVIL
THE CHIEF SPIRIT OF EVIL AND ENEMY OF GOD. OFTEN DEPICTED AS A HUMAN FIGURE WITH HORNS, CLOVEN HOOFS AND A TAIL.

WRITING WHEN YOU'RE LYING DOWN
+ SURFING ON A SEA OF COFFEE
+ ROLLING DICE TO DECIDE WHICH ORNAMENT TO BREAK
+ SLAVISH DEDICATION TO POINTLESS, MENIAL TASKS
+ HORRIBLY FLAWED DESIGNS FOR PLAY EQUIPMENT
+ MAKING A LOG FIRE IN THE OFFICE
+ SURGEON EATING ICE CREAM WITH HIS KNIFE
+ STICK MAN AFRAID OF HAILSTONES AND RAIN
+ FASTEST LOSERS DO BATTLE FOR PATHETIC PLASTIC TROPHY
+ A SLIGHT CRAMPING OF THE BOLLOCKS
AND A SLIGHT RUSTLING OF THE LEAVES
AND WIND-CHIME IN THE GARDEN DRIVING YOU MAD SO YOU HAVE TO GET UP IN THE NIGHT AND SMASH IT WITH A HAMMER
+ DIFFERENCE BETWEEN A TEAPOT AND A COFFEE POT
AND OTHER QUESTIONS DOMESTIC

MENOPAUSE

WHAT DO YOU WANT ?

DO YOU WANT THIS BAG ?

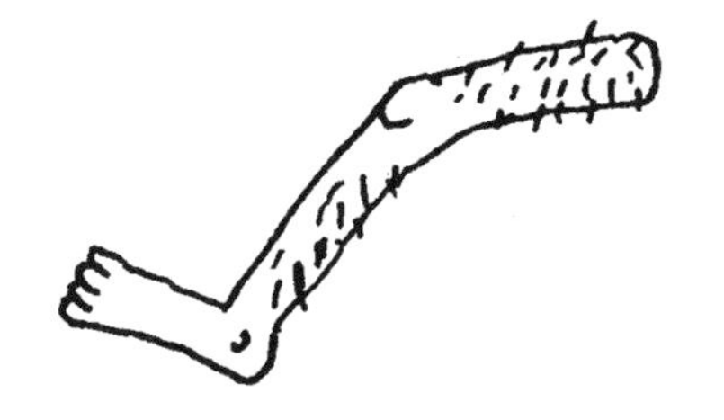

DO YOU WANT THIS LEG ?

DO YOU WANT THIS PIE ?

DO YOU WANT THIS GIANT PAIR OF SPECS ?

DO YOU WANT THIS GARDEN ?

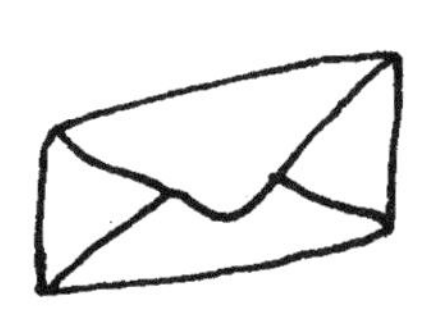

DO YOU WANT THE RESULT OF YOUR TEST ?

— WELL WHAT THE FUCK DO YOU WANT THEN ?

LACK SKILL
LACK PATIENCE
LACK INTELLECT
LACK SUBTLETY
LACK THE POWER OF SPEECH
LACK CONTROL
LACK CONTROL OF MY BODY
LACK AIM
LACK REASON

BUT STILL I WAS ABLE TO GAIN YOUR TRUST

NOW;

YOU LACK ~~[illegible]~~ YOUR LIFE SAVINGS
YOU LACK A MOTOR CAR
YOU LACK MANY OF YOUR POSSESSIONS
YOU LACK TRUST IN OTHERS
YOU LACK THE CONFIDENCE TO LEAVE THE HOUSE
YOU LACK SELF-RESPECT

PLEASE

EAT

US

The oil spill isn't
going to spoil
our holiday

FRIGHTENING ACCURACY

WHEN DUNCAN GOT HOLD OF THE BIG PEN THE PROBLEMS STARTED. PREVIOUSLY WE HAD HOPED DUNCAN WOULD BECOME A DRAUGHTSMAN. HE SHOWED MUCH POTENTIAL, HIS NIMBLE FINGERS RENDERING IMAGES OF TALL SAILING SHIPS AND LEOPARDS AND THE LIKE IN MINUTE AND IMPRESSIVE DETAIL. THEN HE FOUND THE BIG PEN. HE MUST HAVE FOUND IT BECAUSE NO ONE IN THE VILLAGE WOULD HAVE SOLD HIM ONE SUCH WAS HIS REPUTATION FOR CLARITY. WITH THE BIG PEN IN HIS HAND DUNCAN BECAME A MONSTER. HE SCRAWLED MEANINGLESS FILTH WHEREVER HE WAS ABLE. IT WAS A DREADFUL SITUATION. WE ASKED DUNCAN TO GIVE UP THE PEN BUT HE REFUSED, CRAZED IMBECILE THAT HE HAD BECOME.

AFTER DISCUSSION WITH THE VILLAGE ELDERS A COURSE OF ACTION WAS DECIDED UPON. ONE OF DUNCANS FINGERS WOULD BE REMOVED WITH A HATCHET FOR EVERY DAY THAT HE REFUSED TO RELINQUISH THE BIG PEN. DUNCAN HAS NOW GIVEN UP THE PEN AT LAST BUT ONLY HAS HIS RIGHT INDEX FINGER REMAINING. HE CAN NO LONGER DRAW BUT, HOWEVER, HE CAN POINT WITH FRIGHTENING ACCURACY.

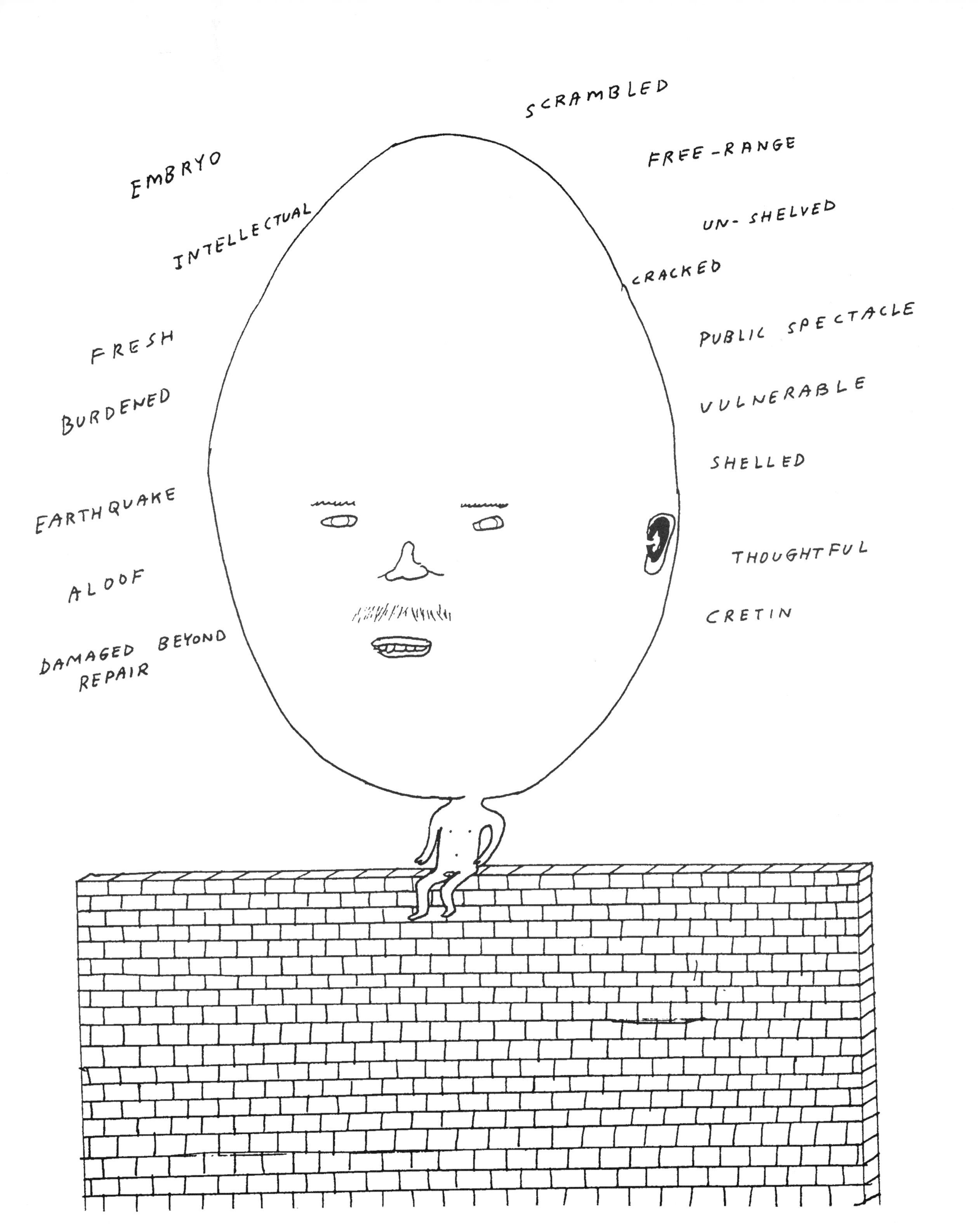
SCRAMBLED
EMBRYO
FREE-RANGE
INTELLECTUAL
UN-SHELVED
CRACKED
FRESH
PUBLIC SPECTACLE
BURDENED
VULNERABLE
SHELLED
EARTHQUAKE
THOUGHTFUL
ALOOF
CRETIN
DAMAGED BEYOND
REPAIR

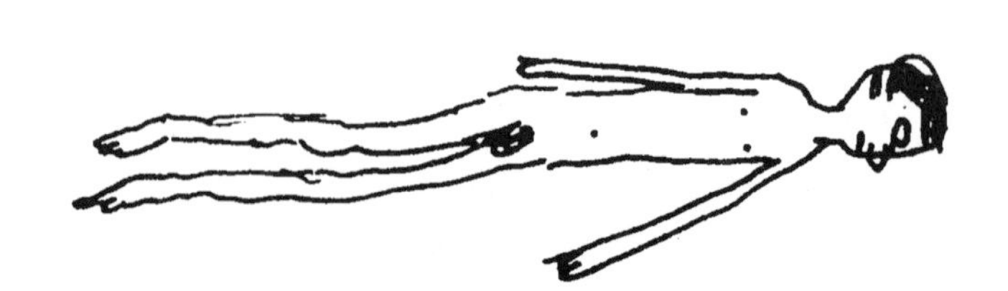

MOM: WHAT WOULD YOU LIKE TO DO TODAY CAMERON?
CAMERON: I WANT TO GO AND SEE THE NAKED MAN IN THE WHEELCHAIR.
MOM: OK.
(THEY DRIVE FOR 20 MINUTES)
MOM: LOOK, CAMERON! THERE HE IS.
CAMERON: BUT WHERE'S HIS WHEELCHAIR?
MOM: I DUNNO.
CAMERON: THIS IS SHIT. LET'S GO. TAKE ME BACK TO MY FOSTER HOME.

I SHALL PROVIDE WARNINGS BEFORE I START TO PUNISH BECAUSE I AM A JUST RULER

- EAVESDROPPERS - WATCH OUT
- PENKNIFE CARPENTERS - WATCH OUT
- COWARDLY BULLIES - WATCH OUT
- QUACKS, CHARLATANS, PHILISTINES, LUDDITES, DESPOILERS OF THAT WHICH WE HOLD DEAR - WATCH OUT
- BLIND DISCIPLES, ETCETERAS, - WATCH OUT
- HIGHWAY FOULERS - WATCH OUT
- GOSSIP MONGERS, FOOLS, - WATCH OUT
- LIARS, CHEATS, THIEVES, - WATCH OUT
- YOU, OVER THERE BY THE FAG MACHINE - WATCH OUT

WHO, ME?

GUTTER IS
BLOCKED WITH
HUMAN FAECES

TINY COW STANDS IN GIANT FIELD. TINY PEOPLE ATTACK AND KILL TINY COW. TINY COW IS DISMEMBERED AND TAKEN TO TINY HOUSE WHERE IT IS COOKED ON A TINY STOVE AND SERVED ON TINY PLATES AND EATEN WITH TINY KNIVES AND FORKS BY THE TINY PEOPLE. TINY PEOPLE SIT AROUND ON TINY CHAIRS. TINY BELCHES ARE HEARD.

GIANT PENIS APPEARS IN SKY ABOVE TINY HOUSE. GIANT PENIS DESCENDS ON TINY HOUSE AND PISSES DOWN CHIMNEY. TINY HOUSE FILLS UP WITH PISS AND TINY PEOPLE ARE DROWNED.

(THIS IS A VALUABLE DOCUMENT. PLEASE RETAIN IT WITH OTHER RELEVENT PAPERS IN A PLACE OF SAFE KEEPING)

TICK ONE BOX

YES	
NO	

"TIMMY"

PIGEONS TIMMY HAS FUCKED:

"SPAM"

"ELAINE"

"BERNARD"

"LITTLE-MISS TURD-EATER"

I'VE STOPPED
DRINKING LIGHTER FLUID

THE HUMAN RACE

EE HOW PEOPLE PREFER LIGHT FROM DARK
EXCEPT ALBINOS)
EE HOW PEOPLE ENJOY OPEN SPACES
EE HOW PEOPLE VALUE PRIVACY
EE HOW PEOPLE LIKE KEEPING PETS
EE HOW PEOPLE KEEP THEIR HOUSES WARM AND TIDY
EE HOW PEOPLE WASH THEIR CLOTHES WHEN THEY ARE DIRTY
EE HOW PEOPLE LIKE FRESH AIR
EE HOW PEOPLE DON'T LIKE THE RAIN
EE HOW PEOPLE OBEY MOST LAWS
EE HOW PEOPLE LIKE TO READ BOOKS AND WATCH MOVIES
EE HOW PEOPLE LIKE HUMAN CONTACT
EE HOW PEOPLE ENJOY THE LIVELY ATMOSPHERE OF SHENANIGAN'S BAR + GRILL
EE HOW PEOPLE SO GRATEFULLY ACCEPT FLATTERY
EE HOW PEOPLE LIKE TO BE BOUGHT DRINKS AND POTATO CRISPS
EE HOW PEOPLE ACCEPT RIDES HOME FROM THOSE THEY HARDLY KNOW
EE HOW PEOPLE WINCE GROTESQUELY AS THE ARE INJECTED WITH POISON
EE HOW THEIR CONTORTED FACES AS THE POISON TAKES EFFECT
EE HOW PEOPLE START TO ROT AND STINK WHEN THEIR CORPSES ARE LEFT LYING AROUND
EE HOW
EE HOW, IN THIS WAY, THE DEAD SEEM TO ANNOY THE LIVING.

BLACK SKY

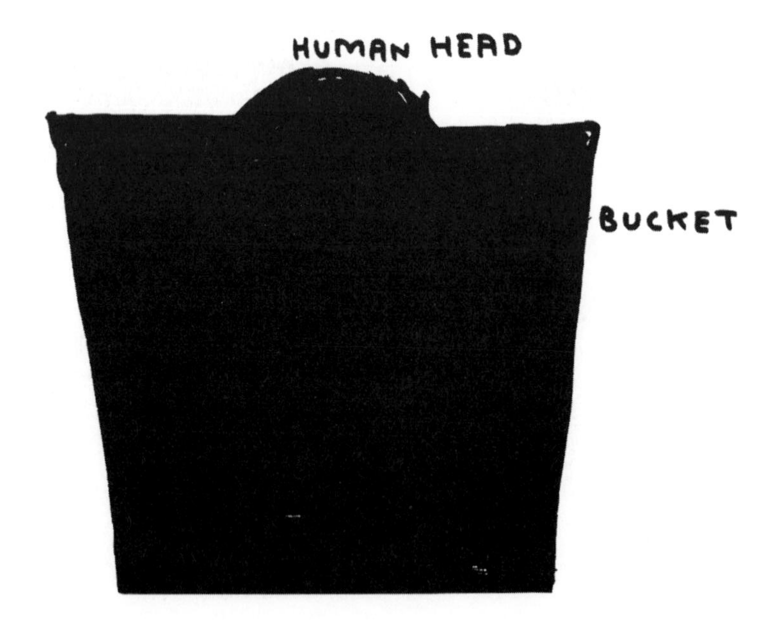

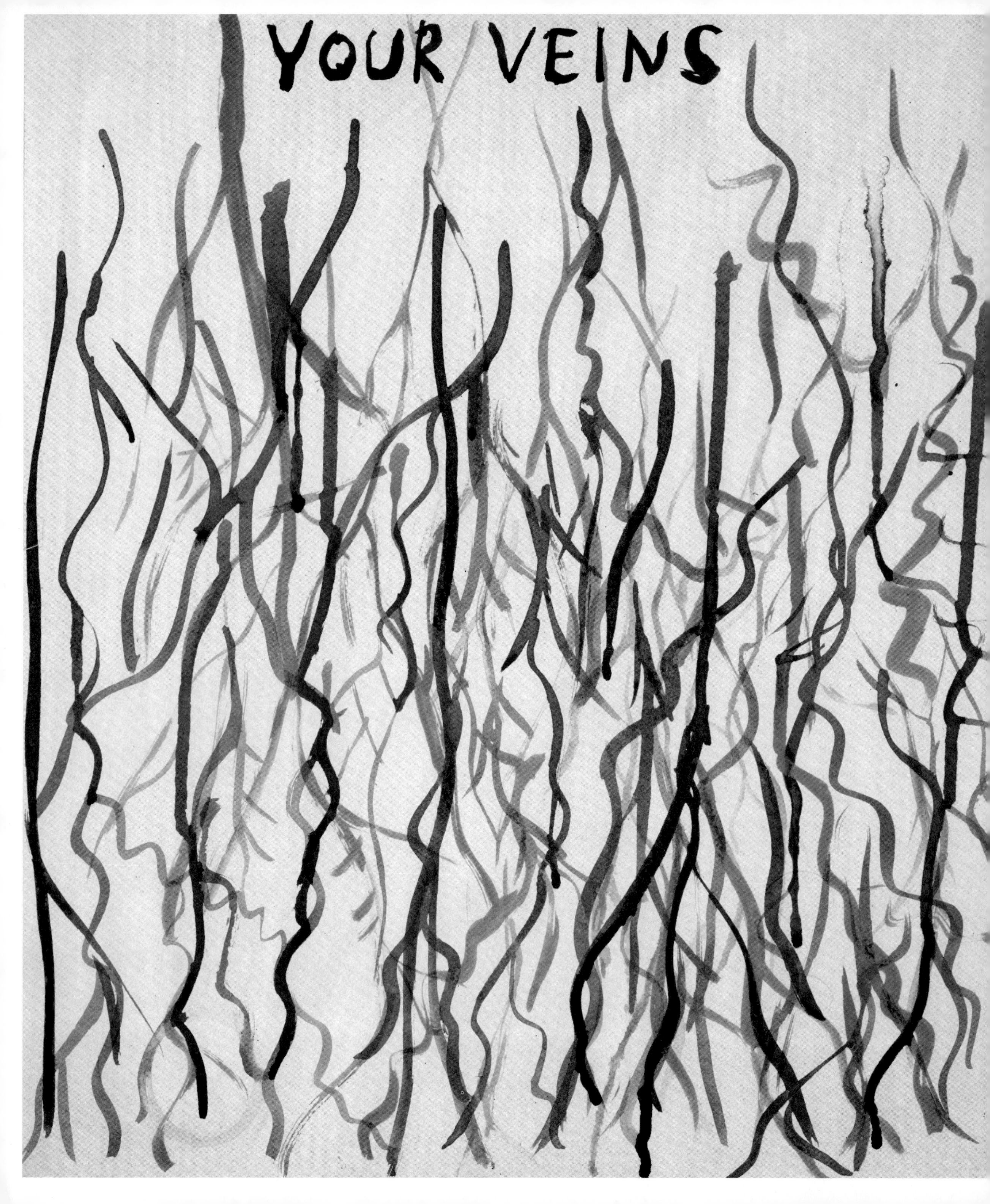
YOUR VEINS

EVERYONE'S
HAPPY

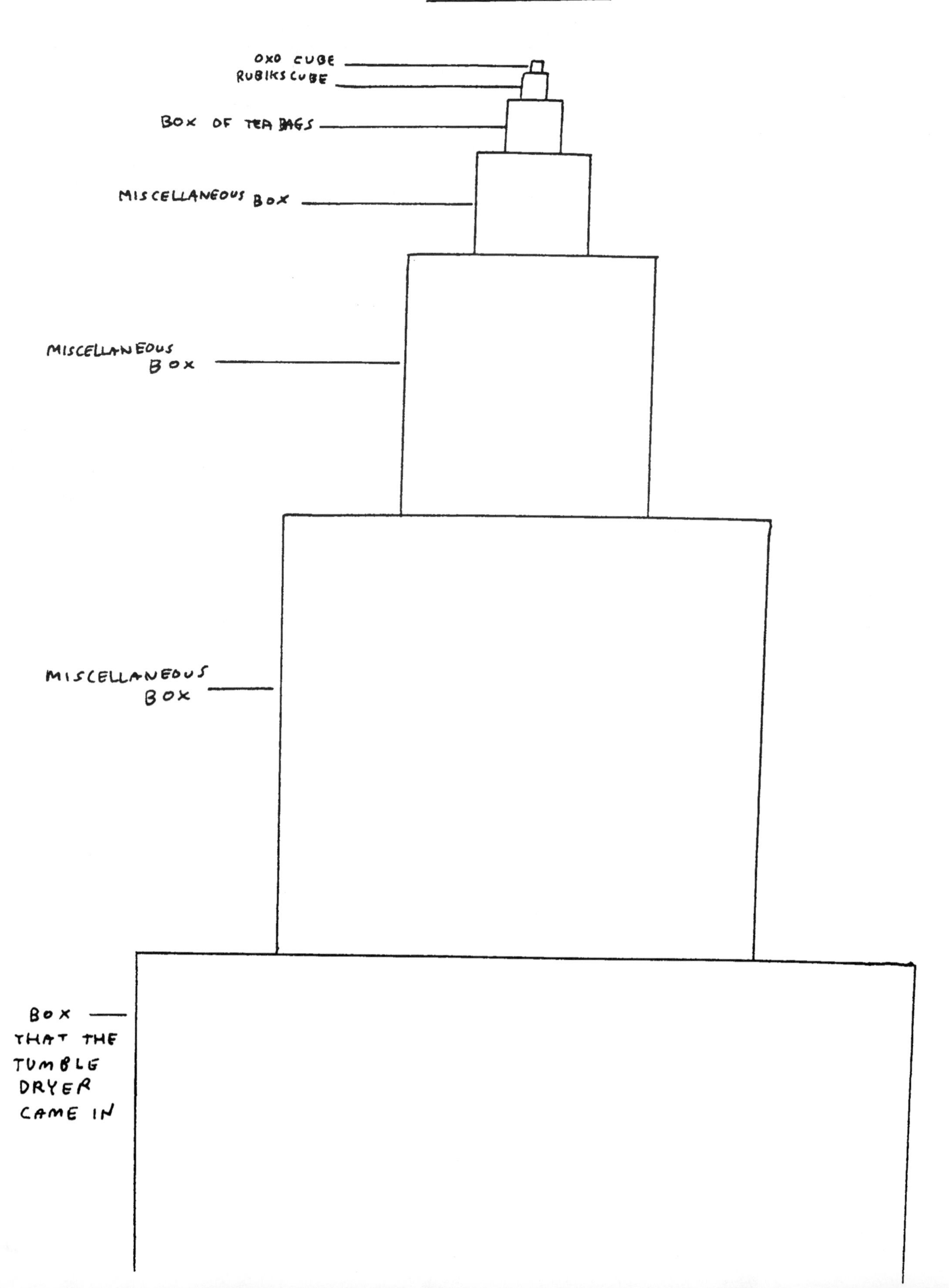
HEIRARCHY
OXO CUBE
RUBIKS CUBE
BOX OF TEA BAGS
MISCELLANEOUS BOX
MISCELLANEOUS BOX
MISCELLANEOUS BOX
BOX THAT THE TUMBLE DRYER CAME IN

(HEAD AGAINST WALL)

BANG BANG BANG BANG BANG BANG BANG BANG BANG BANG BANG
BANG BANG BANG BANG BANG BANG BANG BANG BANG BANG BANG
BANG BANG BANG BANG BANG BANG BANG BANG BANG BANG BANG
BANG BANG BANG BANG BANG BANG BANG BANG BANG BANG BANG
BANG BANG BANG BANG BANG BANG BANG BANG BANG BANG BANG
BANG BANG BANG BANG

(PAUSE)

BANG BANG BANG

(PAUSE)

BANG

(SILENCE)

ROBERT DENIRO
JOHN TRAVOLTA
MERYL STREEP
JULIA ROBERTS
LEONARDO DI CAPRIO
HUGH GRANT
DUDLEY MOORE
DEMI MOORE
ROGER MOORE

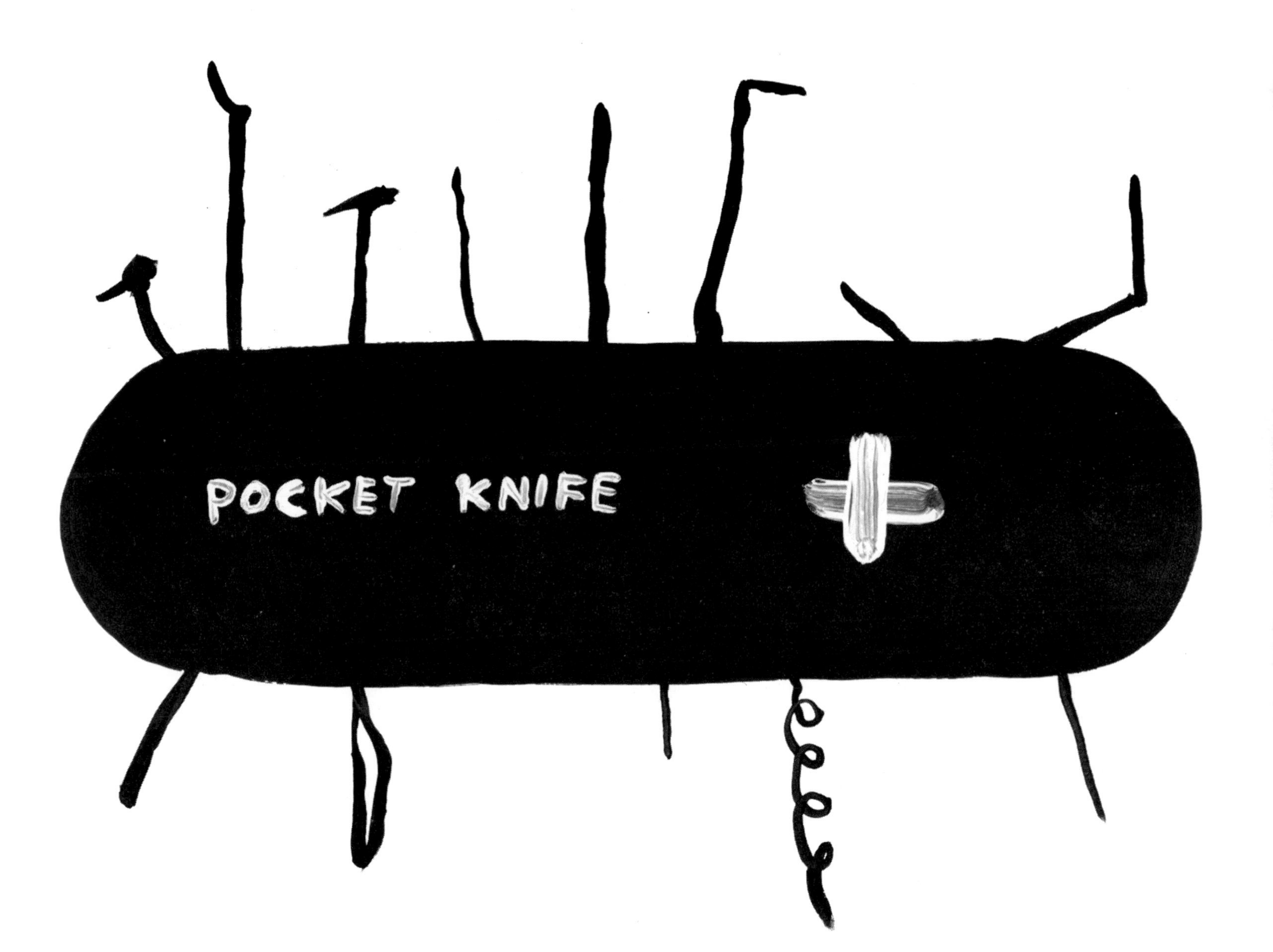
POCKET KNIFE

THIS AFTERNOON'S THOUGHTS (IN ALPHABETICAL ORDER)

1. ALCOHOLIC, THE WANDERER DOES NOT RETURN HE WAS AN
2. COMPUTER, YOUR RELATIONSHIP WITH
3. DEMENTIA, JUVENILE
4. DIRT, OLD LADY IN A FIELD OF
5. EYES, I'VE GOT NUTS IN MY
6. FAILURE, POSSIBILITY OF
7. FAMOUS, HE WROTE DOWN OUR CONVERSINGS AND NOW HE HAS BECOME
8. FLOWERS, AVOID NEGATIVE THOUGHTS, THINK OF
9. FRIENDLY, TRY NOT TO GET TOO
10. GARDEN ORNAMENTS, THOSE TERRIBLE
11. HALVED, YOUR SPIRIT IS
12. HAPPY?, WILL I BE ABLE TO FINISH MY NOVEL ABOUT VIOLENCE IF I SUDDENLY BECOME
13. HELICOPTER, INVISIBLE
14. HOLIDAY, HELP, WE HAVE BEEN KIDNAPPED AN IT HAS RUINED OUR
15. KINDNESS
16. LARYNGITIS
17. LAUGHTER, AUDIBLE SOUND OF
18. LEAF
19. NOTHING
20. ORNAMENT, NEITHER USE NOR
21. PAIN, MY
22. PENIS-BOY, STAY HARD
23. PHANTOM SMELLS: THINGS THAT YOU CAN SMELL THAT AREN'T REALLY THERE
24. ROBOT, YOUR MOTHER IS A
25. SCABS, DISCOVERY OF A CURE FOR
26. SCOTLAND, "IF YOU LEAVE SCOTLAND YOU WILL DIE" MOTHER SAID
27. SEX TOOLS, HOMEMADE
28. SNAILS? ARE THOSE REAL
29. SPONG, THE
30. SPONTO, JIM
31. STOMPING, THOSE BOOTS WERE MADE FOR
32. SUBTLETY: SUBTLETY IS AN OLD FASHIONED VIRTUE. THINGS THAT ARE SUBTLE ARE NOT IMMEDIATLY OBVIOUS BECAU OF THEIR DELICACY OR HIGH REFINEMEN
33. SUPERNATURAL FORCE, BULLETS REPELLED BY
34. THE FOREST FLOOR, DIRT FROM
35. THE TOYS OF THOSE WHO HURT YOU (ALAN, ET AL)
36. TRANSYLVANIA, THE FORMER
37. TWO MICE IN A BAR: FIRST MOUSE "MY WIFE DOESN'T UNDERSTAND ME" SECOND MOUSE "MAYBE SHE'S RETARDED"
38. UGLINESS, THE SOURCE OF
39. ULAN BATOR
40. VAN NUYS AIRPORT
41. WEARY?, WHY ARE YOU
42. WHORES, DEAD
43. WINDOW CLEANER, THE HEADLESS
44. WINK & NOD, COMBINATION OF
45. YOU ARE STANDING WERE I VOMITED.

STEPHEN
HAWKING

HOW WE ARE SOILED

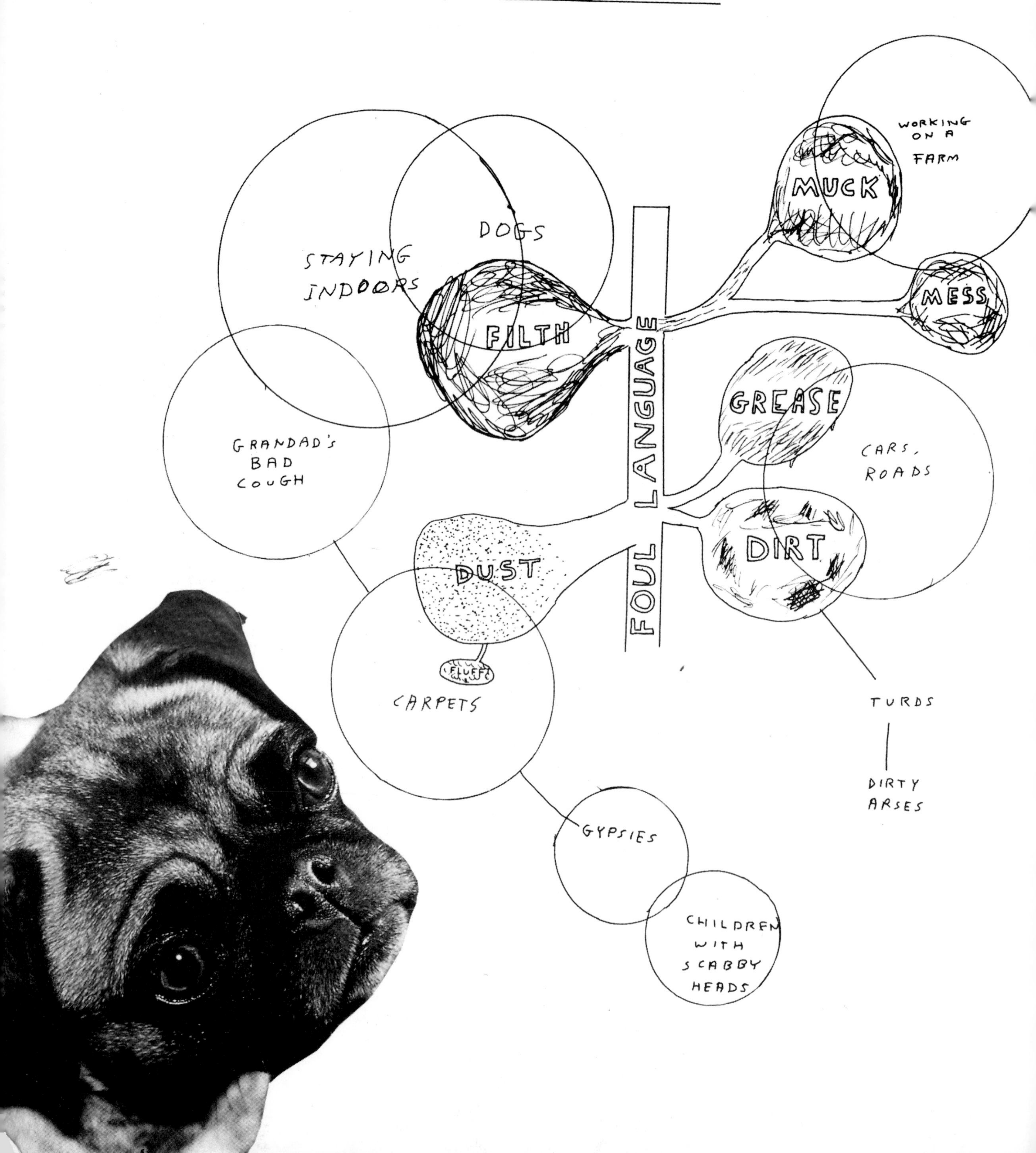

A GIANT PACKAGE IS DROPPED BY AN AEROPLANE ONTO THE BEACH OF A DESERT ISLAND. THE INHABITANTS OF THE ISLAND RUSH TOWARDS THE PACKAGE. THEY ARE V. EXCITED. THE PACKAGE CONTAINS:

HUMAN BODY PARTS PRESERVED IN ALCOHOL. SOILED BED LINEN. SWEETBREADS. APPLES. TOENAIL CLIPPINGS. A SILVER TRUMPET. PEANUTS. ANTIBIOTICS. TINS OF GREASE. STUFFED ANIMALS. A WATERBED. A SAW. A LIGHT. A CHAIR. FACEPAINTS. A BELL. A JAR OF PICKLED EGGS. A BOOK ABOUT WINE MAKING. CRAYONS. A MAGNIFYING GLASS. A 'LIGHT SABRE' (WEAPON USED IN THE 'STAR WARS' FILMS)

WE HATE SCHOOL
IT GIVE US LICE

THE SUBJECT IS MESSED WITH

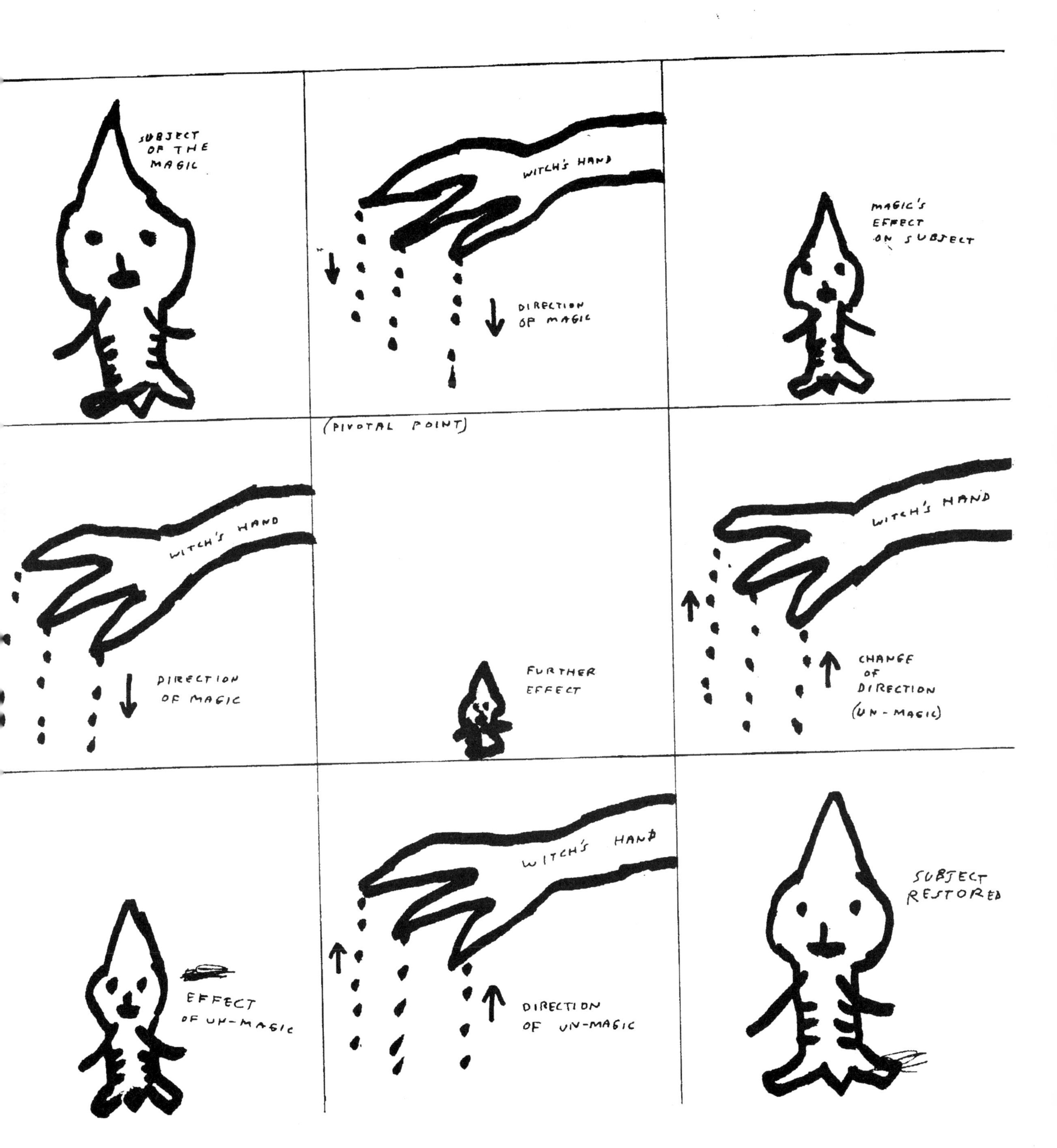

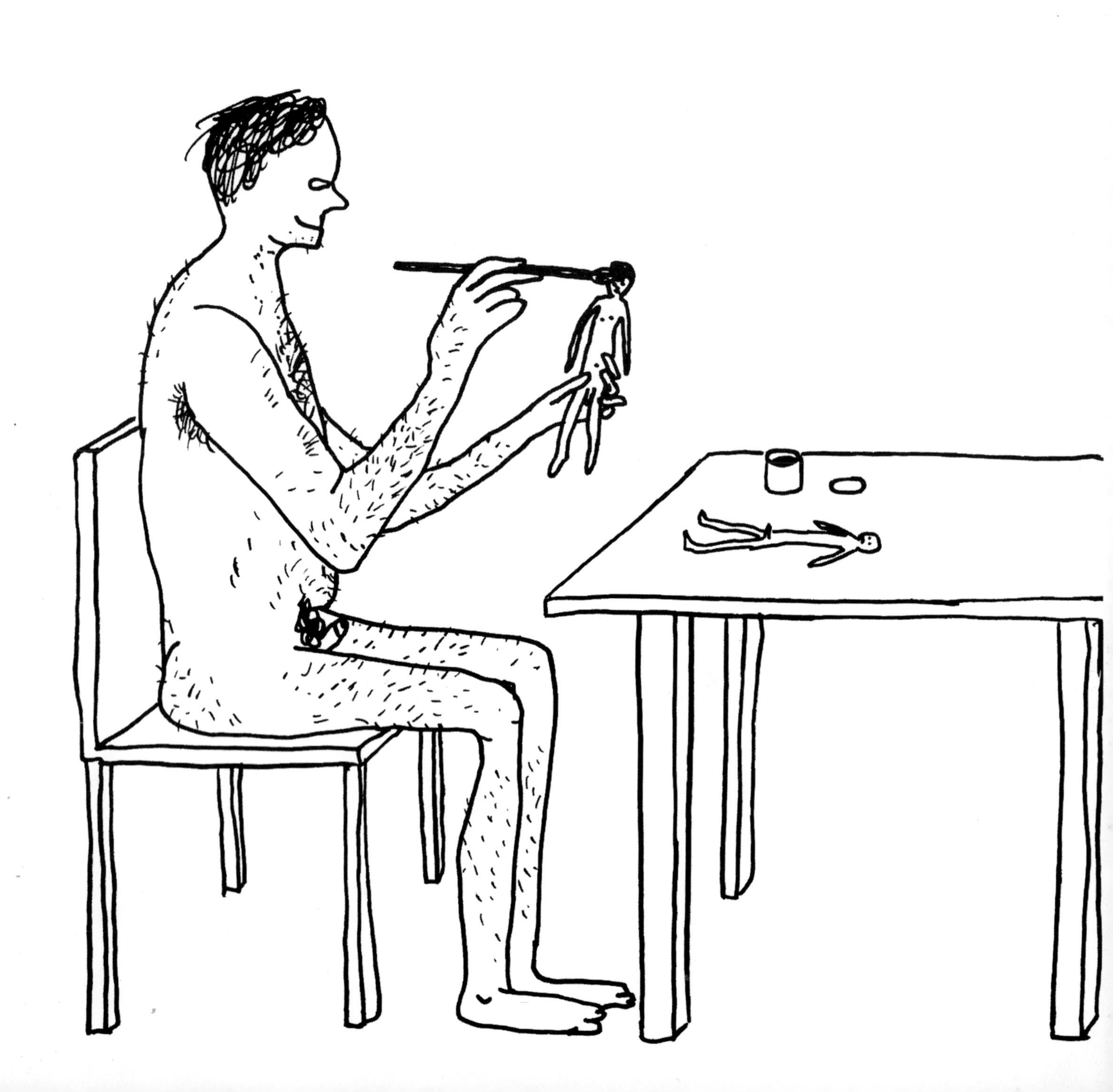

CHILDREN DRESSED AS DEMONS
CHILDREN DRESSED AS DEVILS
CHILDREN DRESSED AS CORPSES
CHILDREN DRESSED AS SKELETONS
CHILDREN DRESSED AS VAMPIRES
CHILDREN DRESSED AS WITCHES
CHILDREN DRESSED AS WEREWOLVES
CHILDREN DRESSED AS MONSTERS
CHILDREN DRESSED AS GHOSTS
CHILDREN DRESSED AS GHOULS
CHILDREN DRESSED AS MURDERERS
CHILDREN DRESSED AS DEATH
CHILDREN DRESSED
CHILDREN
KNOCKED ON OUR DOOR
AND ASKED US FOR MONEY

DON'T WORRY

YOUR WORLD ISN'T FALLING APART

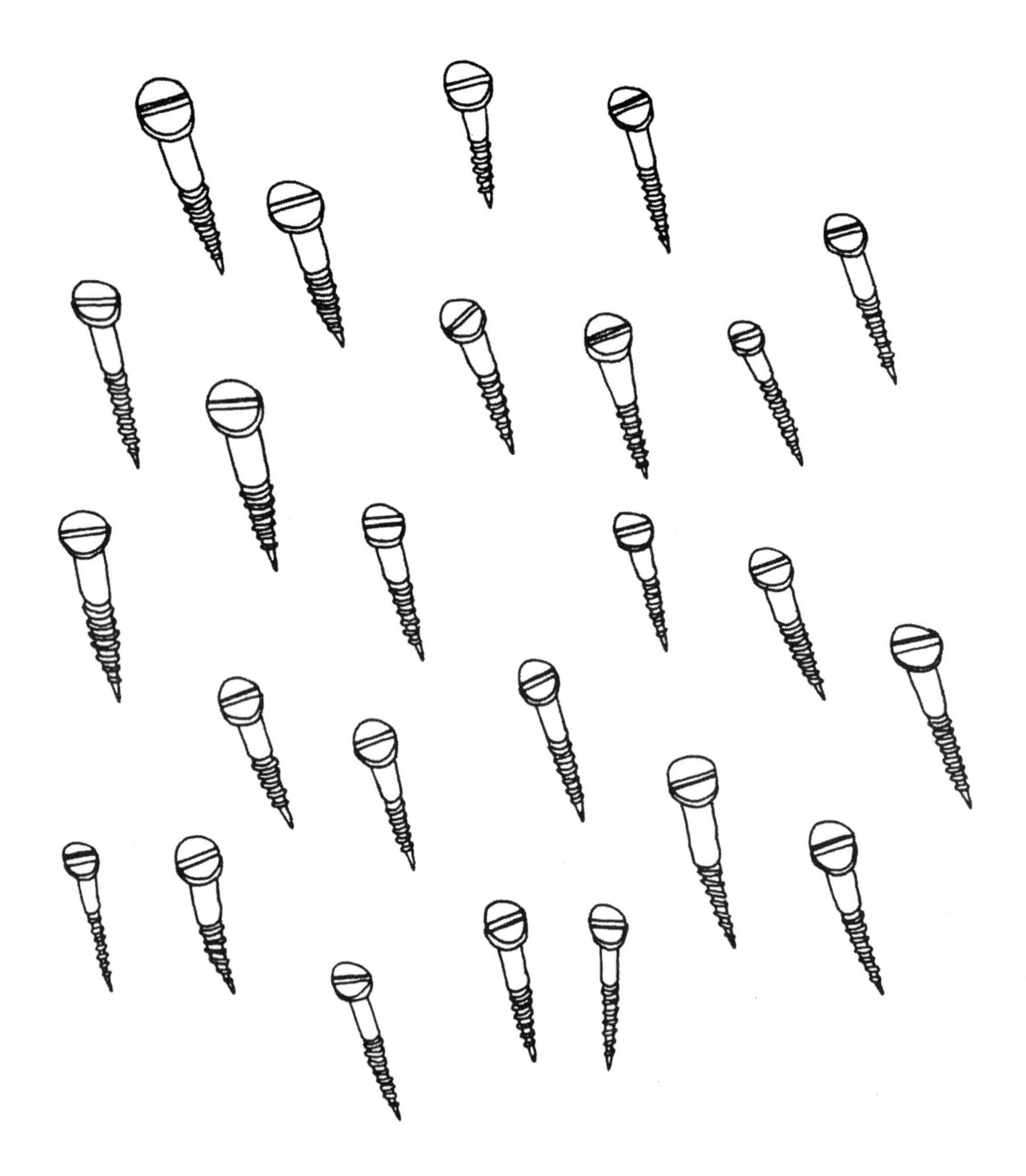

IT'S JUST BEING DISMANTLED

WHY ARE YOU HAPPY ?
BECAUSE I'M FAT

ARE YOU BEING ATTENDED-TO ?

HAPPY
EASTER

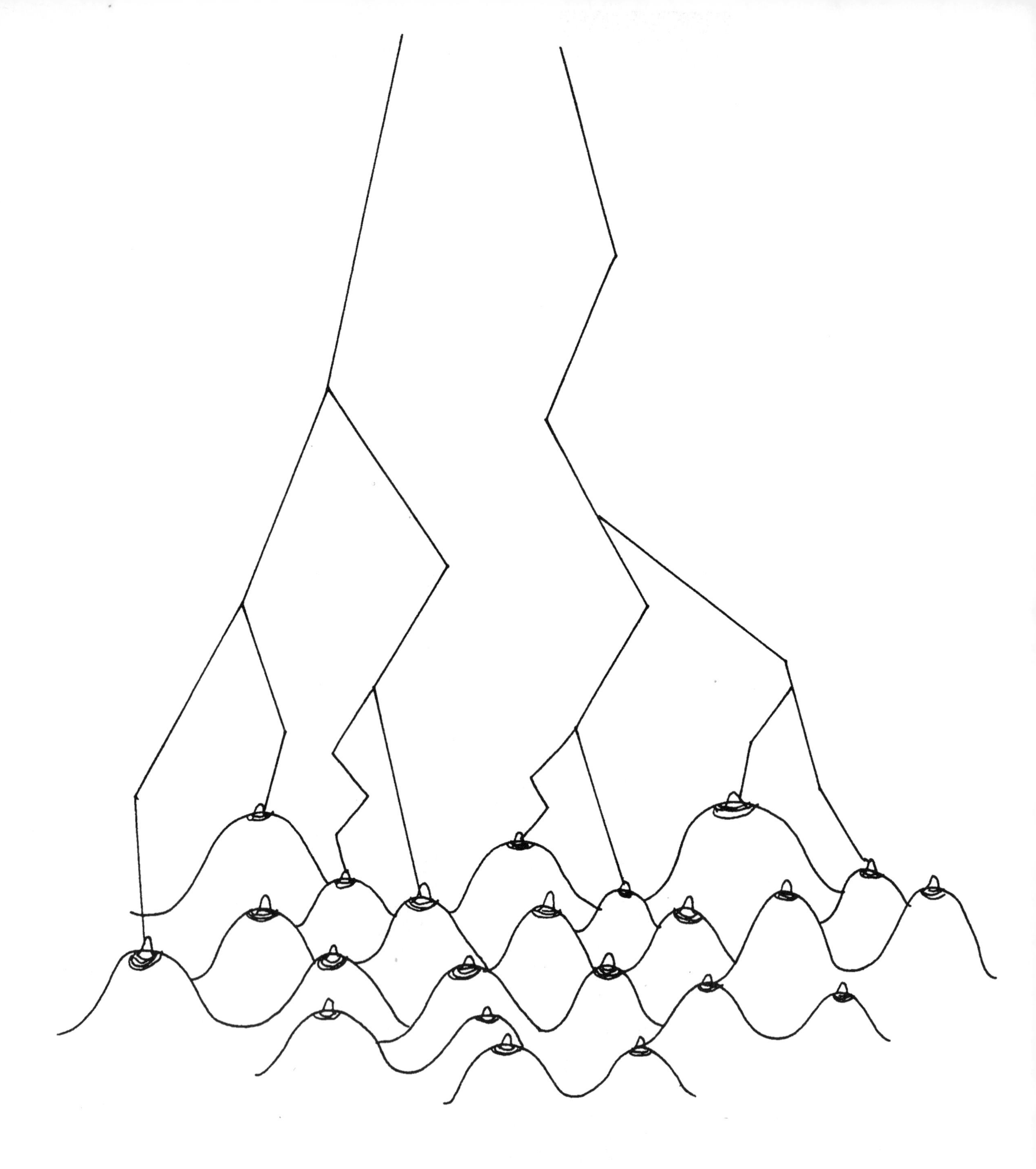
TITS ARE STRUCK BY LIGHTNING

TORTOISE IS BOUND
TO SIGNPOST WITH
STRONG TAPE
ANY OBJECTIONS ?

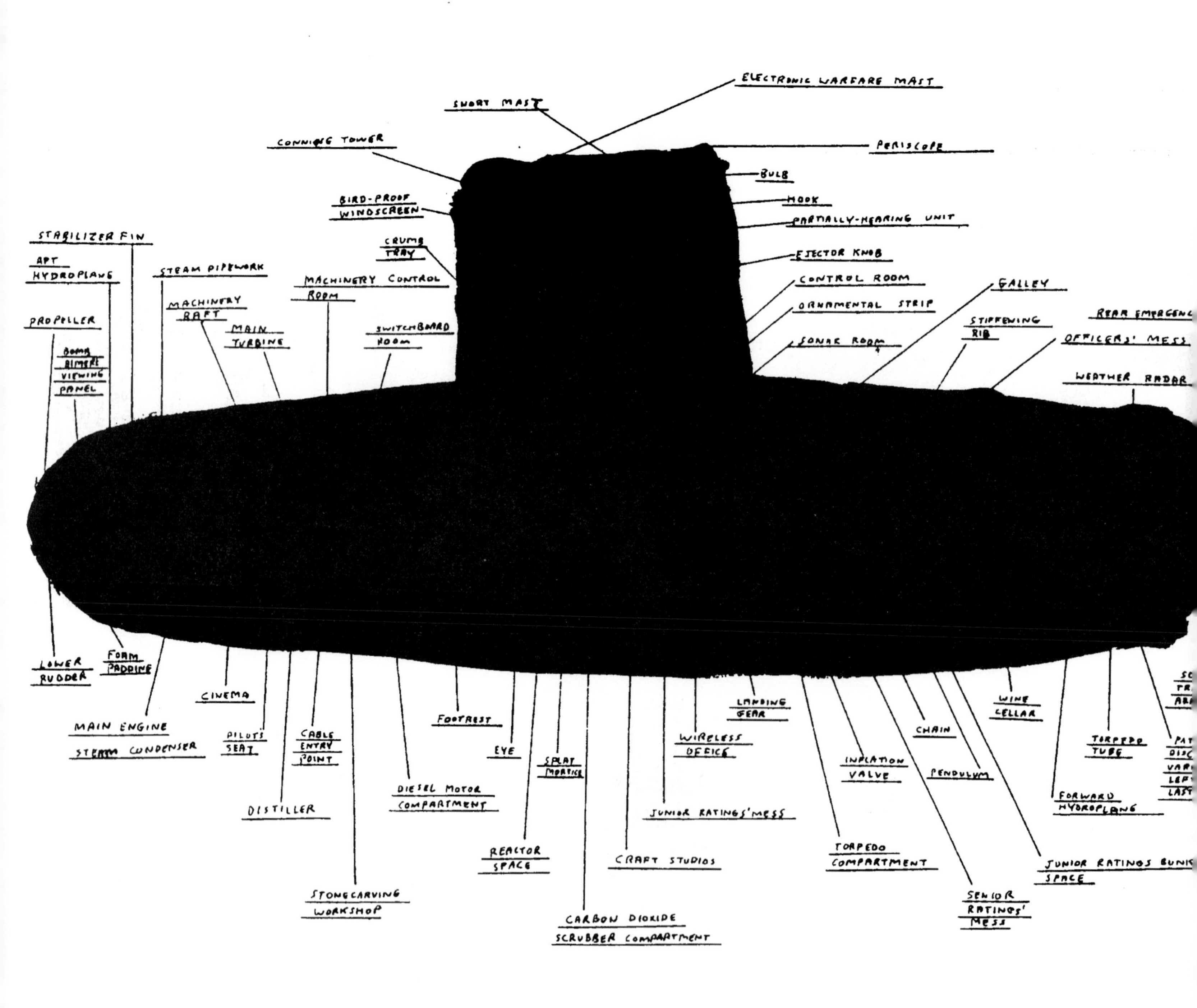
ELECTRONIC WARFARE MAST
SHORT MAST
CONNING TOWER
PERISCOPE
BULB
BIRD-PROOF WINDSCREEN
HOOK
PARTIALLY-HEARING UNIT
STABILIZER FIN
CRUMB TRAY
EJECTOR KNOB
AFT HYDROPLANE
STEAM PIPEWORK
MACHINERY CONTROL ROOM
CONTROL ROOM
GALLEY
MACHINERY RAFT
ORNAMENTAL STRIP
PROPELLER
MAIN TURBINE
SWITCHBOARD ROOM
SONAR ROOM
STIFFENING RIB
OFFICERS' MESS
BOMB AIMER'S VIEWING PANEL
WEATHER RADAR
LOWER RUDDER
FOAM PADDING
CINEMA
LANDING GEAR
WINE CELLAR
MAIN ENGINE
FOOTREST
CHAIN
STEAM CONDENSER
PILOT'S SEAT
CABLE ENTRY POINT
EYE
SPLAT MORTICE
WIRELESS OFFICE
INFLATION VALVE
TORPEDO TUBE
PENDULUM
DIESEL MOTOR COMPARTMENT
FORWARD HYDROPLANE
DISTILLER
JUNIOR RATINGS' MESS
REACTOR SPACE
CRAFT STUDIOS
TORPEDO COMPARTMENT
SPACE
STONECARVING WORKSHOP
SENIOR RATINGS' MESS
CARBON DIOXIDE SCRUBBER COMPARTMENT

SOMEWHAT

DISCONCERTING

POINTED PHALLUS
WITH BLACKENED END

PAY NOTHIN

YOU'RE DEAD

THEN WE WILL CLAIM YOUR BODY
THEN FROM YOUR REMAINS WE WILL BUILD THINGS
KEY RINGS , JEWELLERY
AND WE WILL SELL THEM OVER THE INTERNET
AND PEOPLE CAN BID FOR THEM
LIKE IN AN AUCTION

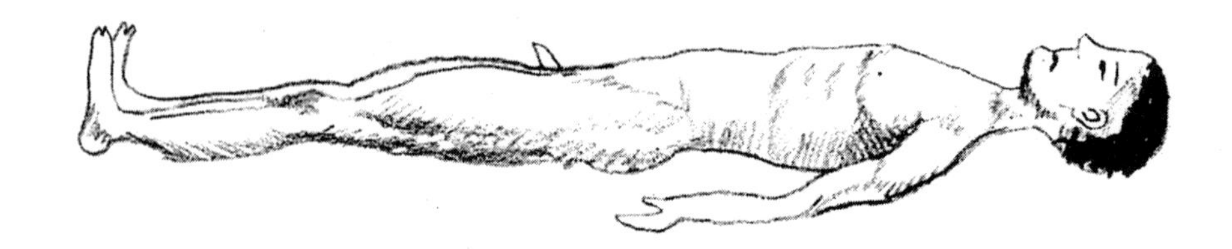

WE
TRY
TO MAKE
EVERYTHING
LOOK LIKE A HUMAN
FACE. THIS MAKES THEM
MORE APPEALING AND HIDES
THE SINISTER NATURE OF THE
IMAGES.

DO YOU LIKE THE PICTURES?
HALF-PAST THREE

HA HA HA HA HA HA HA HA HA HA HA HA HA HA HA HA HA HA HA
HA HA HA HA HA HA HA HA HA HA HA HA HA HA HA HA HA HA HA HA
HA HA HA HA HA HA HA HA HA HA HA HA HA HA HA HA HA HA HA
HA HA HA HA HA HA HA HA HA HA HA HA HA HA HA HA HA HA HA
HA HA HA HA HA HA HA HA HA HA HA HA HA HA HA HA HA HA HA
HA HA HA HA HA HA HA HA HA HA HA HA HA HA HA HA HA HA HA
HA HA HA HA HA HA HA HA HA HA HA HA HA HA HA HA HA HA HA HA
HA HA HA HA HA HA HA HA HA HA HA HA HA HA HA HA HA HA HA
HA HA HA HA HA HA HA HA HA HA HA HA HA HA HA HA HA HA
HA HA HA HA HA HA HA HA HA HA HA HA HA HA HA HA HA HA
HA HA HA HA HA HA HA HA HA HA HA HA HA HA HA HA HA HA
HA HA HA HA HA HA HA HA HA HA HA HA HA HA HA HA HA HA
HA HA HA HA HA HA HA HA HA HA HA HA HA HA HA HA HA
HA HA HA HA HA HA HA HA HA HA HA HA HA HA HA HA HA
HA HA HA

WHAT HAPPENS AFTER YOU'RE DEAD